13 Sinister Stories

Paul Groves, John Griffin and Nigel Grimshaw

Edward Arnold

© Paul Groves, John Griffin and Nigel Grimshaw 1987

First published in Great Britain in 1987 by
Edward Arnold (Publisher) Ltd
41 Bedford Square, London WC1B 3DQ

Edward Arnold (Australia) Pty Ltd
80 Waverley Road, Caulfield East
Victoria 3145, Australia

British Library Cataloguing in Publication Data

Groves, Paul
   13 sinister stories.
   1. Readers–1950-
   I. Title   II. Griffin, John, *1935–*
   III. Grimshaw, Nigel
   428.6   PE1119

ISBN 0–7131–7722–5

All rights reserved. No part of this publication may be reproduced, stored in a retrieval system, or transmitted in any form or by any means, electronic, photocopying, recording or otherwise, without the prior permission of Edward Arnold (Publishers) Ltd

The characters in this book refer to no person either living or dead

Photoset in Linotron Baskerville by Northern Phototypesetting Co.,
Bolton, Greater Manchester
Printed and bound in Great Britain by Richard Clay Ltd, Bungay, Suffolk

Contents

The Lych-Gate 7
The Changing Room 13
Dorkin's Vine 18
Final Departure 27
Reading the Signs 33
The Devil 41
The Red-eyed Cats 53
The Expanding Man 59
The Strange Case of Mrs Harris 64
The Mask 73
Mrs Speckley 78
The Exterminator 86
Thank you, Halley's Comet 95

Also available in the same series:

Titles by Paul Groves and Nigel Grimshaw:
13 Weird Tales
13 Horror Stories
13 Sci-Fi Stories
13 Ghosts

Titles by Paul Groves, John Griffin and Nigel Grimshaw:
13 Computer Tales
13 Family Stories
13 Animal Stories
13 Tales of Crime
13 Stories of Sport and Leisure

To the Teacher

This, like its predecessors, *13 Ghosts*, *13 Weird Tales* and *13 Horror Stories*, contains a further thirteen tales of the horrific, written in simple English to put them within the grasp of the pupil who reads only occasionally or comes to reading with a certain degree of difficulty. Though we hope that each story has sufficient intrinsic interest to be read by the individual pupil for its own sake, each is accompanied by questions which point the way to written work or discussion. The first series of questions examines the reader's comprehension of the story and can usually be answered by reference to the text. The second set asks about the wider implications of the tale and refers to the pupil's own experience. Then there is a section on language generally, usage, meaning, and orthography. Finally come suggestions for written work ranging from the formal to the more imaginative.

The Lych-Gate

1.4.87

Dear Mary,

I am writing this down and dating it to show that what has happened to me is not fanciful. In the future, perhaps, some scientists of the mind will be able to explain it. I want to say here and now that I am not the seventh son of a seventh son; there is also no history of such things in our family. I also want to assert most forcibly that I have had nothing to do with the powers of darkness. I am a practising Christian and I have always had an abhorrence and dread of any trappings of the Devil. I worship regularly and try to lead a Christian life. So why has this power been given to me, for I do see it as a power?

As you know the lych-gate of our church in Lower Babbington is a pretty one. It is built of sturdy oak struts and beams and its roof has deep red pantiles that glow in the sunsets over Locking Hill. Some past carpenter of the village put great love into it which has made it much photographed today. I had planned to have our wedding photos taken round it.

Mary, my only love, now you are reading this you will understand the sadness that has been in my heart and why I went away so suddenly. I was desperate not to hurt you but I had to go. I knew you would think I had fallen out of love. But I loved you all the more, dreading what planned ecstacy I should now miss. I apologize, Mary, for the hurt I have given you, but I could not bring myself to tell you of my fears. You might have left me, thinking me mad.

It started in January. I came out of church one morning after the communion service. I walked down between the yews of the churchyard path. Ahead of me under the lych-gate was Mrs Simons, the church treasurer. I knew it was her because she turned and smiled. I hastened my step because I wanted to see her about the coming jumble sale. She had not been in church so it was odd that I should now see her leaving. I thought she might have been on some business in the vestry and was too busy to take communion. As I reached the lych-gate she had gone; the lane to the right and the left was empty. I thought perhaps she had been whisked away by her husband in his car.

I called at her cottage on Tuesday thinking no more of the incident. Her husband came to the door. He said his wife was not well but would see me. She was sitting in her arm chair by the fire under a travelling rug. She said her stomach was playing her up again which was why she was not in church on Sunday. I blurted out that I had seen her under the lych-gate after morning communion. She said that she was in bed at the time.

I laughingly said that she must have a double, though my laugh was mechanical as I began to doubt my own sanity. I would have sworn on the good book that I had seen her. It was daylight after all. And as I left I saw the coat and hat she had been wearing hanging in the hallway. I put it from my mind as the week got busier at work. Then on Saturday the phone rang. It was her husband. Mrs Simons had died in the night.

Three weeks later I was going to evensong. Normally you would have been with me, dear Mary, but you were away visiting your aunt. Ahead of me, under the lych-gate, I saw Mr Pearson, the vicar. He turned and smiled at me. I waved. As I reached the avenue of yews he had gone on quickly into the church. Inside I sat in my usual pew as I waited for the service to commence.

I was surprised to see a new young priest come out of the vestry. I waited for Mr Pearson to follow but he did not come. Later in his sermon the young priest said that Mr Pearson had a heavy cold and was at home in bed. The rest of the sermon and service went right over my whirling brain. I knew I had seen our vicar under the lych-gate. Although it was dark it was well lit for the old people. I paused there going out as if it could reveal its mystery to me. Then I went home and did not sleep well. It might have been different if you had been there to confide in.

On the Tuesday morning I was woken by the tolling of the church bell. My mother came in. The vicar had died in the night from pneumonia. I did not go to work that day as my experiences of the lych-gate shut out all other thoughts. I told my mother I had a migraine. Had I the power to know who would die next in our village?

I visited the lych-gate six times during the day, pretending to take a walk for my migraine. I looked it up in the church guide. It said it was where the coffins used to rest on the way to burial. This confirmed in my mind that it was not imagination. There was some aura of death about it. In my febrile mind the smiles I had been given by Mrs Simons and Mr Pearson now seemed the toothy smiles of a skull. In February I saw two more people under the lych-gate after morning communion – Miss Atkins and Mr Summer. Neither were church goers so they would not normally have been there. They had both vanished when I reached the lane. Both were dead within six days.

I wondered whether to tell you, my darling. Perhaps if you had been with me I might. I wondered, too, whether to tell the bishop for as yet we had no new vicar. But I decided this dreaded secret could only be borne by me. For some reason I had been given this 'gift' and I must suffer it alone. Now you know why I did not always answer your questions and you got cross with me.

I bought Danny in March, as I thought people would think me odd always walking round the church. Now I had an excuse to walk him four times a day. You see I could not keep away from the wretched lych-gate. My work suffered and I was given a warning by my boss.

Then today, the first of the month I saw it. Oh God, does it have to be the first of April? Is it some great celestial joke?

On my third walk of today I saw a figure under the gate, a tall figure. It turned and smiled a skull-like smile. I could not believe what I saw. My heart palpitated like mad. It was myself!

I turned and ran home stumbling over Danny as he got between my legs. I rushed past my mother and ran up to my room. She is outside now calling. I shall say nothing to her. I am writing this all down so quickly. Please do excuse the handwriting. I am posting it to my solicitor today. Then I am going away. I cannot say where. But if I do not return within seven days or he hears of my death he will send this to you.

I love you always. Oh, my darling, how I love you.

Richard

Footnote: Richard Clare was killed in a motor accident on the 2nd of April 1987 on his way to Bournemouth.

Think It Over

1. What is a lych-gate?
2. What is a 'practising Christian'?
3. Who is Mary?
4. Who did Richard first see under the lych-gate?
5. What happened to her?
6. What is a vestry?
7. Why was Richard surprised to see a new young priest come out of the vestry?
8. What showed that the vicar had died?
9. How many 'apparitions' did Richard see under the lych-gate?
10. Why did Richard not tell Mary what was happening to him?
11. Why did Richard buy a dog?

Think It Out

1. What powers is the 'seventh son of a seventh son' supposed to have?
2. Why would photographers want to use the lych-gate as a background?
3. What is 'the good book'?
4. When did you guess that Richard might see himself, or was it a surprise?
5. If it is so frightening, why does Richard visit the lych-gate so much?
6. How would you classify this story? Is it a ghost story?

Using Words

1. Use 'play' or 'playing' with as many different meanings as you can in sentences of your own.
2. What is the difference between 'practice' and 'practise'?
3. The word meaning 'having foresight' begins 'presc....'. Look it up in a dictionary.
4. These words from the story are misspelt. Find them and correct them: abhorence; desparate, extacy; wisked; traveling; pallpitated.

Discuss Now

Have you ever had to keep a great secret you could not discuss with anyone?

If you had been Richard, would you have confided in a priest? Richard in his letter says 'I am not the seventh son of the seventh son; there is also no history of such things in our family'. What is the significance of this superstition? Has anyone any evidence of superstition being justified? What makes people superstitious?

Write Now

1. Write the report of the police officer called to investigate the death of Richard Clare. He will have interviewed Mary, and seen the letter.
2. Write a letter to a friend about something odd you thought you saw, but were not sure.
3. Write as a play the conversation Richard has with Mrs Simons.

The Changing Room

The girls got off the bus at St Nicolas's Convent School laughing and giggling. This merriment hid the inner tension. This was going to be a tough match. The winners would be top of the hockey league for local schools. As far as the William Morris Comprehensive School was concerned it was more than tough: no visiting team had won on the St Nicolas's ground for 5 years.

Two nuns greeted the team together with their captain. 'We thought you might like a cup of tea first,' said the smaller one. Her face looked doll-like under her veil.

'Oh, lovely,' grinned Miss Arnold, trying to hide her own feelings of inferiority as she looked round the splendid new buildings of the convent school. 'Jennifer.'

Jennifer came forward and shook hands, first with the nuns and then with their captain. 'How old is the convent?' she asked.

'It was begun in the 14th Century,' the smaller nun said. 'But of course bits have been added ever since. The sports facilities were added just 5 years ago. We may be an old order but we must keep up to date.'

The taller nun smiled. She appeared to have no conversation. They went down a cloistered path into a large refectory. Great oak tables and benches smelling of beeswax stood reflecting the colours of the stained-glass windows high in the room. Blue mugs were placed in line down two of the tables. A nun stood with a large teapot smiling. Jennifer drank hers quickly.

'I'll show you the changing room,' said the small nun to

13

her. Her skin was like a cream advert, yet her lips were thin. 'No need to bother the others yet. You can show them the way.'

She lead Jennifer back down the cloisters. 'You're the goal-keeper I believe?' she said.

'Yes,' said Jennifer.

They came to a door marked *'Changing Room'*. The nun opened it and held the door for Jennifer to walk in. To Jennifer's surprise she did not follow her but closed the door.

Jennifer looked around. It was like a normal changing room with long benches and grey steel lockers. It was 'T' shaped. At the end was a large mirror. Round the left corner were some sumptuous showers, and round the right was a couch. Everything was clean and spotless. Not a hint of mud and not a whiff of sweat or shoe smells.

'I'll get the others,' Jennifer thought. She turned round.

To her surprise a 'T' shaped room faced her. There were the long benches and the lockers, but instead of the door she had come in on the left there were the two arms of a 'T' shaped room.

Perplexed she went to the end. Round one corner were the showers. There was no door out. Round the other was another 'T' shaped room. She swung round. There was no couch but another 'T' shaped room. Jennifer was not given to fanciful thoughts. She was a tough girl which was why she was captain and played in goal. Her heart beat fast. What was happening to her? Had the tea been drugged? Was she hallucinating?

She ran to the end of the room she was facing. She looked quickly left and right. Each time she saw two 'T' shaped rooms of identical pattern. She ran to the end of the left one and hammered on the wall in frustration. She hardly dare now look left or right, but when she did so two 'T' shaped rooms faced her.

Her mouth tasted of phlegmy dryness; her breath came fast. Memories of being lost in a maze in Hampton Court as a four-year-old flooded her mind. She sat on a bench.

Then she got up and ran, taking left turns each time as she came to the end of each 'T'. Faster and faster she went, letting out the kind of cry you might hear in a jungle late at night. As she passed the mirrors each time she could see that her face was whiter than the nun's.

Finally, she collapsed in a sobbing heap by her bag. Her mind twisted like an unending spiral staircase of fear. Then greyness.

The small nun was picking her up. 'Are you all right, my dear? Just sit there. I'll get your teacher.'

Jennifer clung to her. 'Don't go!' she sobbed.

The nun firmly pushed her off. She had surprising strength. 'I'll get your teacher,' she said firmly.

Miss Arnold rushed in. 'What is it Jennifer?'

'I must have passed out, Miss.'

'I'll get the school nurse,' said the small nun.

'No, I'm all right.'

'Has this happened before?' asked Miss Arnold.

'Never, Miss.'

'Well, you can't play now.'

'Oh, I must, Miss.'

The nurse came. She examined Jennifer. 'I think she's all right. The excitement must have got to her.'

'Oh, please let me play. I am the captain. The team needs me.'

'Well, as you are in goal, Jennifer. But if you feel faint you must leave the pitch.'

Jennifer changed into her kit. She felt shaky but said nothing. They would think her mad, if she told them about the room. She still made sure she was not the last to leave it.

Jennifer let in two goals near the start. She would normally have saved them but they slipped through her shaky hands. St Nicholas's won 3–1.

Think It Over

1. Why would it be a tough match?
2. Why might Miss Arnold feel inferior?
3. What is a refectory?
4. What are cloisters?
5. What is a T-shaped room?
6. Why did Jennifer collapse?
7. Why might the nurse over-rule Miss Arnold?
8. Why did Jennifer not tell of her experience?
9. Why did the William Morris school lose the match?

Think It Out

1. Explain the title of the story.
2. What is slightly creepy about the small nun?
3. What is 'an old order'?
4. Why is the story more creepy for taking place in an old convent?
5. What is the first odd thing about the changing room?
6. What was the most frightening thing about the changing room?
7. Could the tea have been drugged? Give a reason for your answer.
8. Is there any evidence that the same experience happened to other visiting captains?

Using Words

1. Use 'change' in two different ways in sentences of your own.
2. Use 'veil' and 'vale' and 'faint' and 'feint' in sentences of your own.
3. What words show Jennifer's fear?
4. Use the following in sentences of your own: passed out; passed over; passed by; passed on.

Discuss Now

How do players behave and feel before an important match?
What childhood experiences still flood into your memory?
Why is the story all the more odd for taking place in a convent?

Write Now

1 Jennifer has to go back into the changing room at the end of the match. Write about her feelings as she does so.
2 Write as a play. After the match Jennifer tells Miss Arnold of her experience. How does Miss Arnold react?
3 Describe your own school changing room in a paragraph. Pay particular attention to the smells.

Dorkin's Vine

When Jason Martin's parents went abroad, he moved in with his uncle, George Dorkin. Uncle George, being the rich owner of a large house, had a lady who came in to do the cleaning and washing and another who came in to cook.

This state of affairs pleased Jason who liked bed and a quiet life. He was not, however, idle. Much of his time was taken up with thinking about his poetry. Tuesday was his busy day. Then he would make the long trip into town to draw his unemployment benefit. At other times he also did small jobs for his uncle who would reward him, absent-mindedly, with fivers. Jason had no rent to pay.

It would have been an ideal life for Jason but for one thing. His uncle was mad about flowers and plants. There was a large conservatory, a long, glassed-in room at the back of the house. That was full of plants. Every other room in the house, not forgetting the bathroom, had several plants in it. At the end of the garden, well-stocked with plants, was a wooden summer house. There was also Uncle George's potting shed and a laboratory where he did his experiments.

The laboratory gave Jason the creeps. Uncle George referred to his plants in there as 'exotic species'. He'd invented them all and to Jason they were weird. There were plants with tendrils which clutched things. There were plants in bright, diseased-looking colours. There were even plants which ate things. Uncle George doted on them all. He bred them and fed them and watered them and mated them and was always creating new varieties.

He talked about them, too, all the time. Whenever he and Jason met for meals, he would go on and on about plants, sometimes using words that Jason didn't know and never stopping to explain. Only plants. Jason would try to put in a remark about something he had heard on the radio or what it would be like if anyone ever published one of his poems. Uncle George ignored him and went steam-rolling along about his plants.

'The Giant Redwood or sequoia semper virens, as you know, my boy,' he said, 'has an immensely long life span. That is one of the fascinating things about plants – some have a capacity to survive for great periods of time. Almost immortality!' He made a gesture and knocked over a cup.

Here we go again, thought Jason, setting it right. Uncle George lectured on, staring at him glowingly. 'In fact,' he said, 'I am making an intensive study of that kind of thing. I have collected plants from all over the world which live apparently for hundreds of years.'

Jason listened, drawing patterns on the table-cloth with the end of a fork.

Uncle George had mated several of these long-living plants and come up with a species of vine. It was his theory that the juices of this vine, given to a living animal, might prolong its life amazingly.

'I have some May-flies for this,' he told Jason. 'May-flies, as you know, my boy, live only for a day. Within the week, I shall be ready to feed them a concoction I shall prepare from the vine. I expect them, after that, to live for a month, or longer.'

He had cleared all the plants out of the conservatory and installed the vine in there. 'It is a fast grower and already flourishing,' he explained. 'It will need plenty of room. And I have decided I can't wait for it to flower and fruit. It is doing so well that I am going to rush things slightly. In a day or two, I shall clip some lengths from its taller, juicier stems. The sap from those, I am sure, will give me what I want. Exciting, isn't it, my boy?'

'Very,' Jason agreed.

He was horrified when his uncle was found dead. It was Mrs Needham, the cleaning lady, who discovered the body. She looked into the conservatory, saw Uncle George lying there, and screamed. Jason rushed in, tried to revive him, found it was no use and sent for the doctor.

The doctor decided that Uncle George had broken his neck after falling from a ladder.

'He must have got up the ladder to chop away at that great big plant thing with his shears,' said Mrs Needham, still white and shaking. 'It looks just as if it wrapped one of its tendrils round the foot of the ladder and pulled it over to stop him!' she breathed.

Jason looked at her pityingly but the remark triggered something off in his mind. He'd been fond of his uncle and had never liked any of the plants. He couldn't believe that the vine had pulled the ladder over. But if Uncle George had not been up there finding out what the plant juice might do to May-flies he would still be alive. You could say that plants had been the death of him.

Jason brooded about it and things came to a head in his mind after the harrowing moments of the funeral. A lust for revenge flared within him. He didn't know who now owned the house or the plants. He didn't care. Alone, that evening, when the cook had gone home, he gathered together all Uncle George's strongest weed-killers and other poisons. He mixed these up into several gallons of a very potent brew and watered every plant in the house, giving a particularly lavish dose to the vine. Next day, all the plants were either dead or looking very sick and droopy.

'Poor things,' said Mrs Needham. 'They must be pining for poor Mr Dorkin.'

'Yes,' agreed Jason, who had given a second enormous dose to everything the evening before.

'That vine, though—?' said Mrs Needham, wonderingly.

'I know.' Jason nodded thoughtfully.

The vine had taken all that Jason could give it and thrived. It was hard to understand. He'd even mixed it a special potion of lavatory cleaner and paraffin, seeing that it seemed to revel in ordinary poisons. It had revelled in the lavatory cleaner and paraffin as well.

It was – disturbing. Jason had been into the conservatory more than once just to study it. You could almost have kidded yourself that you could see it growing. You could have guessed that it had been created by a man with an unusual mind. It had a thick, fleshy, yellowish stem, big purplish leaves which reminded Jason of bruises and tendrils speckled pink and brown.

He worked on it for a week, first giving it fierce mixtures of his own invention and then spending some of his dole money to buy a bottle of what the man in the shop said would kill oak trees. He soaked the vine in that. The vine lapped it up.

One Saturday afternoon he sat for a long time in the conservatory, glaring at it. It seemed to flaunt its power, challenging and taunting him. By that time, it covered all three walls of the room, most of the roof and was hanging across part of the door.

Was it unstoppable, unkillable? Had Uncle George succeeded only too well? Jason pondered.

He was, however, a determined young man not given to despair. I'll burn it, he thought. It may not be mine to burn but I don't care what anyone says and I'm not going to be beaten by a plant. First chop all the branches down.

Carry them out into the garden to dry. Then burn them. Then dig up the roots and burn those, too.

He was just getting up to go and find the tools for the job when he felt a touch on his ankle. He looked down.

'Hey!' he yelled, jumping up. A tendril of the vine had wrapped itself round his leg. He tore himself free and reached the door.

It was not easy to get out. While he had been deep in thought, other tendrils had apparently spread themselves across the door and twined round the handle. It took a lot of strength to tear them free but finally he slammed the door behind him, locked it and leant against it, panting.

What on earth had Uncle George done? Was the vine not only almost unkillable but capable of thought as well? Could it now be after him because he had tried to poison it?

'I wouldn't bother cleaning the conservatory,' he told Mrs Needham on the Monday.

'Oh, I don't,' she said. 'I daren't. That plant frightens me. Huge, ugly thing. Do you know it's broken two windows? It's climbed out and it's starting to grow up outside the house.'

That did it. Fear now fed Jason's hatred of the thing. Armed with a pruning saw, a sickle, a pair of shears, secateurs and an axe, he burst into the conservatory, hacking, hewing, chopping and slashing.

The result was a draw. Jason did cut off a few branches and ripped away several tendrils but, as the vine by then was almost filling the place, it was like cutting through jungle but worse. The vine did seem to have a mind of its own. One tendril snatched away his saw while others went for his arms and legs. Jason had so much to do freeing himself with the secateurs that he had no chance to swing the axe and far less to get near one of the main stems.

Branches lashed him across the face and he was driven back and forced to use the sickle on the door just to get out.

That night Jason was fortunate. He had taken the shears up to his bedroom by mistake. It was a hot summer night with a bright moon. He was suddenly awake with a sense of something wrong.

He sat up in bed to see a stem of the vine swaying towards him from the window. At the end of it, about the size of a saucer and funnel-shaped was a sucker. Just before it could hover over his head, Jason slid like lightning sideways and on to the floor. It weaved after him. He dodged. It came again cutting him off from the door.

Then he remembered the shears. He found them on a chair, lopped off the sucker and then went back towards the window, heedless of the way the stem tried to lash at his head, clipping it into little bits.

Later he found that one of the branches that had broken its way out of the conservatory through a window had wormed its way round the house and climbed up as far as his bedroom. With a struggle, he cut the whole thing off just outside the conservatory window and hacked it all into bits, too.

Burning the lot next morning gave him a splendid idea.

In the potting shed, among a pile of other things, he found a flame-thrower that Uncle George had used to keep down weeds. Jason bought four gallons of paraffin and surged to the attack, armed with the flame thrower and a large garden spray.

With the flame thrower lit, he opened the conservatory door, squirted a flood of paraffin inside and then went in, turning up the flame thrower to full blast. The result was spectacular.

Within seconds the place was a mass of flame. Windows cracked like rifle shots, the branches of the vine, blackening and withering, lashed about in tongues of fire. Jason squirted in more paraffin and kept the flame thrower roaring. Unfortunately, the vine, writhing in its death throes, drove him back with blazing branches. Jason, in fighting these off on the other side of the door, set fire to some curtains and a chair in the big drawing room.

As it turned out, when the will was read, Uncle George had left most of his money to Kew Gardens and the rest of it to Jason's parents. The house and all its contents he had given to Jason.

It was a fine old house with plenty of oak panelling but a very long way out in the country. By the time Jason had decided he couldn't put the fire out himself and summoned the fire brigade, the whole old, dry place had burned to the ground.

The vine was destroyed which was a good thing. The house was fully insured which was another.

Jason, though, had no end of trouble with the insurance company. They insisted that, on the evidence, Jason had started the fire deliberately. Jason had to fight his case through the courts. Everybody looked doubtful when he talked about the vine. The whole thing ran on for weeks with regiments of lawyers on both sides and in the end the insurance company had to pay up. It was a hefty sum but there was only just enough to pay all Jason's huge legal fees.

In a way the vine seems to have struck back at him for what he did to it, leaving him poor. He thinks about it quite a lot.

What if one tiny bit of the vine was not destroyed? What if, even now, that bit is quietly putting forth roots, preparing to grow giant-like and take vengeance on mankind for what it has suffered?

Sitting at nights in his lonely bed-sitter, Jason is not easy in his mind.

Think It Over

1. How had Jason come to live with Uncle George?
2. What did Jason do every Tuesday?
3. What didn't Jason like about Uncle George?
4. How did Jason feel about Uncle George's plants?
5. Why did Uncle George grow his vine?
6. What happened to Uncle George?
7. How did Jason revenge himself on the plants for Uncle George's death?
8. How did the vine react to Jason's poisons?
9. What did Jason decide to do at first after that?
10. How did the vine react to Jason's failed attempt to chop it up that night?
11. How did Jason finally get rid of the vine?
12. What else was destroyed as well as the vine?
13. Why didn't Jason get any insurance money?
14. What does Jason worry about now?

Think It Out

1. What in the story suggests that Jason is rather lazy?
2. What suggests that Uncle George is only interested in his own ideas and opinions?
3. Who was right about the cause of Uncle George's death, Jason or Mrs Needham? Explain why you think so.
4. How do you know that Jason must have been quite fond of his uncle?
5. What else besides long life had Uncle George's experiment given to the vine?
6. What do you think the vine would have done to Jason if it had caught him in his bedroom?
7. In what way had the vine struck back at Jason as he killed it?

Using Words

1. Explain the difference between a conservatory, a green house and a potting shed.
2. What is the difference between a tendril and a tentacle?
3. 'Uncle George lectured on, staring at him glowingly.'
   What does the word glowingly indicate about how Uncle George felt?
4. Jason had some harrowing moments at the funeral. What sort of moments are 'harrowing'?
5. 'You could almost have kidded yourself that you could see it growing.' 'He had no end of trouble with the insurance company.'
   The underlined words are slang. Replace them with one or more words that are not slang.
6. What are 'death throes'?

Discuss Now

Are all scientific discoveries and inventions for the good of mankind? Can you think of some that are and some that are not? Or, are scientific discoveries neither good nor bad? Does it depend on how they are used and who uses them?

Write Now

1. Write your own story about a dangerous plant.
2. Jason is right. A small piece of vine blows away into an old lady's garden. She, a keen gardener, waters it and feeds it. It begins to grow. What happens after that?
3. In play-form write the scene in court where a lawyer for the insurance company tries to make Jason admit that he burnt the house down on purpose and Jason tries to explain what really happened. Remember it might be hard for Jason to make people believe in the vine.

Final Departure

Foster found himself out in the country, wondering how he had got there. He must have had another of his 'white-outs' as the doctor had called them. Foster had stopped worrying about them. They had been happening so often. They were all part of the stress he was under. He could do nothing about that.

It had all started some months ago when his printing business had started to fail. He had worried himself into a black depression. He had become very short tempered and forgetful even then. He had tried to shake himself out of it by driving himself too hard. But he had simply driven himself into the doctor's surgery.

'These pills will help,' Doctor Capes had told him. 'They'll calm you down. I don't think they'll help with your lapses of memory, though.'

They hadn't. He kept having periods of time which were complete blanks. He would find himself parking the car in a street with no recollection of how he had got there. No. Not with no recollection. He could always back track in his mind and slowly remember.

That is what he ought to be doing now, not standing by this gate staring into a field with a blank mind. So – he had set off late, in a mad rush, to get the car in for a service. Yes, he remembered driving fast through the lanes. Obviously he had handed the car in at Chapman's garage and then, presumably, sunk deep in his worries, he had wandered out here into the country instead of going into town.

But – no, he had better not start brooding over the little gaps, the little details that still escaped him. Act, the doctor had said. Don't keep turning worries over and over in your mind. That makes them worse.

He should have gone to the bank. That was it. Macauley, the manager, had wanted to talk to him about the interest on his loan. He couldn't pay. He didn't want to see Macauley. It could be that some part of his tricky mind, wanting to postpone that interview, had taken him away from town. And that was silly. It would do no good to avoid Macauley. He'd better get it over with.

He started to walk quickly back into town along the road. Was he starting with flu on top of everything else? He felt muzzy. The cars that passed him sounded muffled as if they were a long way off or he had something wrong with his hearing. Could that be a side effect from the pills? He'd better see the doctor again. Still – he shouldn't be thinking about that now. What was he going to say to Macauley?

Beside the car park he stopped. Chapman's was just down the side street. Should he call in to see that he really had left his car for its service? No. He'd look ridiculous going in and asking questions like that.

As he was about to move on, a dog came trotting round one of the parked cars. When it saw him, it stopped dead. Its hackles rose, its lips went back over its teeth and it snarled. Foster shrank back in alarm and then, in a sudden spasm of irritation, he stamped his foot and growled back at it, 'Get away, you stupid animal!'

It flinched, low on the ground. Then it turned and ran off with its tail between its legs, making a sound between a snarl and a whine. Angrily Foster looked round for something to throw after it but then he shrugged and walked on.

The bank was fairly full with queues at all the tills. He threaded his way past these and went to the back where he pressed the bell to call one of the assistants. The clock on the back wall said 11–15. His appointment with Macauley had been for eleven.

People in the queues paid in or drew out money and left. Others came in so that the queues didn't shorten noticeably. The buzz of conversation behind the counter among the clerks was dull, like the sound of the cars on the road. Foster realised he had been waiting, in a kind of dream for almost 5 minutes. Impatiently he pressed the bell button again. Still no one came. He stabbed the bell two or three times without result. A man at the end of the nearest queue looked at him. Foster scowled and said, 'They certainly take their time here, don't they?'

The man stared back expressionlessly and didn't answer. The queue moved on and he looked away. Foster grunted at the rudeness and put his hand flat on the bell, keeping it there. Then he leaned over the counter, trying to catch the eye of one of the clerks. 'Excuse me,' he called aggressively. 'Can you help me?'

They still ignored him.

'Excuse me,' he called even more loudly and stepped back glaring about him in irritation just in time to see Macauley on his way out of the bank.

'Macauley!' he called, really furious now. 'Mr Macauley! Just a minute!'

Macauley made no sign that he had heard and slipped quickly out of the front door.

Foster's anger faded to be replaced with a feeling of emptiness. What did it matter whether he saw Macauley or not? He knew what Macauley would say. Pay the interest or we'll take immediate steps to recover our loan. Pay the interest? He hadn't the slightest chance of doing that.

For a moment he stood there in the bank, at a loss and unable to move. He knew, though, why he felt empty. Rushing into town that way, he'd missed breakfast. Well, the morning had turned out to be a fiasco. He would go and have a cup of coffee.

He made his way to the cafe above the confectioners. He knew the place well. He had often talked to Linda, the rather vague waitress, who had told him about her visits to seances and her interest in the spirits.

As he climbed the dark stairs, Linda came out of the back kitchen up there carrying a tray. She was about to cross the corridor at the head of the stairs when she looked down and saw him.

She glanced and then stared, her expression one of pure terror. He heard the cups, plates and saucers make a gentle jingling on the tray as her hands shook. At a loss, he took two more steps and came to the top of the stairs.

His movement seemed to unlock her stillness. 'Oh, My God!' she breathed in the faintest of whispers and backed slowly through the swing door into the kitchen, the tray making a harsh clash as she disappeared.

Her going uncovered the mirror set in the corridor to throw light down the dark stair. He saw his reflection, not normal, not smartly dressed and combed. There was blood and hair across his face; the suit was torn and filthy. There was blood on that, too, on the chest.

The stairs, the mirror blurred and vanished. He moved blindly somewhere at intense speed. Then he could see again.

Below him, he could see black tyre-marks on the road. There were gashes of fresh earth on the grass verge and a gap torn in the hedge. On its side in the field was a car he recognised, a wreck. On the road he could see a police car and an ambulance.

Just before the ambulance man drew the red blanket over the dead face of the body on the stretcher, he saw it clearly. It was his own.

And then, suddenly, he was in a different place altogether, somewhere he had never been before.

Think It Over

1. What was Foster wondering about when the story opens?
2. What had he been given to help him with his depression?
3. How much could he remember about his journey?
4. Where was he supposed to go that day?
5. How did the dog frighten him?
6. What happened when he spoke to another man in a queue at the bank?
7. How did Mr Macauley annoy him?
8. What interest of hers had Linda, the waitress, told him about?
9. How did she feel when she saw him?
10. When did he first begin to realise what might have happened to him?
11. Where did he go immediately after that?
12. What did he see lying on its side in a field?
13. Whose body was it on the stretcher?
14. Where did he go after that?

Think It Out

1. What did the doctor mean by 'white outs'?
2. In the 5th paragraph what suggests he might have had an accident?
3. Why was the dog frightened of him?
4. Why might the sound of traffic and conversation in the bank have sounded muffled to him?
5. How was it that only Linda saw him?
6. '. . . suddenly, he was in a different place altogether . . .' Where do you think he was?

Using Words

1. The first and last letters of each of the words on the following page are given together with their meanings. Write out the words from the story, being careful to get the spelling right and then use each word in a sentence of your own.

31

l....s	breaks in something that happens
r..........n	remembering something
p........y	supposedly, probably, in a way expected to happen
m.....d	dull sounding, not heard clearly
s...m	a sudden sharp attack

2 'Act, the doctor had said. Don't keep turning worries over and over in your mind. That makes them worse.' Write this out punctuating it as the actual speech of the doctor.
3 What is the 'interest' on a loan.
4 What is happening if you 'flinch'? How might you feel if you 'shrug'?

Discuss Now

Do most accidents happen because of a momentary loss of attention and are they unavoidable? Or are they due to ignorance of danger? Are there things that could be done to prevent them in the home, on the roads and at work?

Write Now

1 Write your own story about the difficulties caused by someone's sudden lack of memory. It could be slight or it could be serious.
2 Write the newspaper account of Foster's accident. Make up a headline for your story.
3 Linda, the waitress, does not know at the time that Foster is dead. Write, as if you were Linda, what she might say to a friend when she reads the account of the fatal accident in the newspaper.
4 If we have an after-life, what will it be like? Write about someone discovering this after death. It could be Foster in the story.

Reading the Signs

'Can you see him?' said Mrs Watson anxiously.
Madame Clara cupped her hands round the crystal ball and gazed into it.
'Can you?' insisted Mrs Watson.
Madame Clara let the suspense build up. Then she nodded. 'He's in a street,' she whispered. 'He's crouching in a shop doorway. He holds a rifle.' She narrowed her eyes and fell silent.
'What's happening?' implored Mrs Watson. Madame Clara looked up and stared unseeingly at Mrs Watson for a long moment. 'I can see no more,' she breathed.
'Oh!' The sound was like a moan. Mrs Watson pulled herself together. 'Is he – is he coming home?' she asked. Madame Clara closed her eyes as if what she had done had exhausted her powers.
'For that we need to read the cards,' she murmured. She handed Mrs Watson the pack. Mrs Watson shuffled it with eager fingers and laid a sequence of cards out on the table. Madame Clara studied it. 'He is coming home,' she prophesied.
'Oh.' This time Mrs Watson sighed in relief. 'Home. Safe?' she enquired.
Madame Clara nodded.
Mrs Watson fumbled in her handbag. She pulled out a scrap of handkerchief and blew her nose. She lifted her glasses to wipe her eyes. 'Soon?' she asked and Madame Clara nodded again.
'Oh, I'm so glad. So glad,' Mrs Watson rejoiced. She scrabbled in her bag for banknotes and pressed them on

Madame Clara. Madame Clara thanked her with cool dignity.

As Mrs Watson babbled her thanks, Madame Clara shepherded her to the door. She left at last and Madame Clara went back to her small, green cloth-covered table where the cards lay with the crystal ball and laughed.

What a fool!

Mrs Watson's son, David, was in the army, serving in Northern Ireland. It hadn't been hard to work that out on their first meeting. After that it had been standard procedure. You simply told Mrs Watson what she longed to hear. Of course, you wrapped it all up in a bit of mumbo-jumbo to make it sound mysterious but, once a mark was hooked it was all plain sailing.

Absent-mindedly, Madame Clara picked up the pack of cards, turned them over and put them down. The bottom card lay face upwards. It was the ace of spades. She glanced at it without interest.

It was astonishing, she thought, how many fools there were in the world, how simple they were and how they wanted to be deceived! Make two or three probing suggestions, study their reactions and you knew all you needed to know. On Mrs Watson's first visit she had not even had to do that. Guessing from Mrs Watson's anxious face, she had said, 'You are worried about a loved one.'

'Yes,' Mrs Watson had blurted. 'He's in Belfast.' You didn't have to be even half way clever to work that out.

They were mostly like that. They paid well to be conned. Madame Clara smiled, shaking her head. Old Mrs Marsh had been so impressed by Madame Clara's 'second-sight' that, apart from all the fees she had paid, she had left Madame Clara ten thousand pounds when she died. The thought brought Madame Clara's mind back to important matters and she went upstairs, carrying Mrs Watson's banknotes, to put them in the cash box hidden on top of the wardrobe. The box had slipped, somehow, right to the back and, as she lifted it down, clumsily because she stretched, she knocked down, too, a dusty, old, flat cardboard box which spread its contents across the floor. These were a sheaf of old photographs, one of which slid clear from the rest.

'Well, I never!' Madame Clara picked it up and studied it. It was a picture of herself, younger, standing beside a much older woman.

'Granny Lee,' she marvelled.

The old woman had been a fortune teller, too. Granny Lee, though, believed in the fortunes she told. She thought she did have the gift of real second sight and she told people only what she truly saw in their future.

Granny Lee, you might say, had shown Madame Clara the wrong way to go about things. Madame Clara had decided to go her own way, the proper way. Granny Lee hadn't approved of that. They had drifted apart.

Madame Clara thought about that as she put the money away. She slipped the photograph back among the others and stowed the cardboard box away on top of the wardrobe.

'Granny Lee!' she shook her head pityingly. The old lady had died poor.

And yet – the memory stayed in her mind when she got downstairs. Granny Lee had been right. Madame Clara did indeed have the gift. She could see into the future. It didn't happen often but now and again she had this – this – what? A visitation? She would feel cold, a little light-headed, a little strange and she would see strange things.

Once, with a client she had seen a small child in the crystal ball in what seemed to be a hospital bed. Another time she had seen a noose of rope. She hadn't been able to explain either of these visions. The two clients had been upset when she described them. They hadn't come again. There had been other occasions. None of them had been profitable. In time Madame Clara had abandoned any attempt to understand them and after that, ignored them.

Why, then, did the memory of Granny Lee make her so uneasy now?

She sat down at her green-covered table and her eye fell on the cards. Her uneasiness grew. The ace of spades?

Feeling half-foolish and half-frightened, she told her own fortune. What she read from the cards made little sense. She dealt and read them twice. The only sequence that seemed to have any meaning was the ace of spades – again – and, repeated with it a two, a six and a five. Annoyed with her own jumpiness but compelled, she consulted the crystal ball and, as she did so, that old chilly, light-headed feeling went through her.

She saw ice. Images came and dissolved. Icicles hung from gutterings. Fish lay in chunks of broken ice. A cloud drew a blanket of whiteness over grass. A window pane was starred with shapes. A pond was skimmed with a thin glittering surface.

'Ugh!' She sat back, closing her eyes. When she looked again, the crystal ball was only glass.

She went into the kitchen, rubbing her arms to drive away a shivering that didn't come from cold, and poured herself a large drink. It calmed her fears.

She sat there and thought.

It would be dangerous not to heed the warning. But what did it mean? The calendar on the wall caught her eye. Was that it? It was Wednesday, the twentieth of May. Might two, six, five be the twenty-six of May, the fifth month? The thought reassured her.

The meaning of the ace of spades was clear enough. The death card. She shivered again.

Working out what the crystal ball had indicated took longer.
Ice. Things freezing. An icy road? In May that was unlikely. Still, she wouldn't go out at all next Tuesday. The refrigerator whirred suddenly, startling her. Was that it? She liked a few gin and tonics at night with lemon and ice. An ice cube could choke you. She'd do without gin next Tuesday. She wouldn't eat any frozen food, either.
Her decisions calmed her but not completely and her tension grew during the next few days as the possible significance of the warning went round and round in her mind. She was glad to have clients. Dealing with them in her old well-tried way took the edge off her problem. Naturally, she cancelled all appointments on the Tuesday to be on the safe side.

The whole day was nerve-racking. She ate little and spent most of her time wandering apprehensively from room to room. The worst moment was when an ice-cream seller parked outside. She sat trembling, looking out of the window, until he left.
That night she lay awake, quivering as midnight came and passed. Then she dozed, plagued by nightmares.
When she got up late on the Wednesday morning she was dizzy with relief and a whirl of other emotions. What a fool she had been! And what a drivelling old fool Granny Lee had been! What kind of second-sight was it that showed you only meaningless nonsense? A gift, indeed!
Joyful relief, though, conquered all else. She would go into Swanton, the next town and give herself a good time.
It was a glorious day with the blossom coming on the trees. By the time she reached Swanton, it was opening time. She went into the Black Swan and had a good many gins to celebrate. When she came out she was chuckling

to herself. Cards? Numbers? What rubbish!

'And there was nothing frozen. Nothing! No danger at all,' she sneered aloud to the empty pavement and hiccupped. Unsteadily she stepped out into the road from behind a parked delivery truck.

They did what they could for her but it was no use. As they put the body into the ambulance, the patrol policeman was taking details from the driver of the white van who had had no chance to brake. The van had a logo on the side, a playing card. Above that it said, 'The Ace of Spades Restaurant' and below it gave the phone number, 'Swanton 265'.

'Name, sir?' demanded the policeman.

'Alan,' said the driver who was still white and shaking. Then, realising how silly that sounded, he added, 'Alan Frost.' He cleared his throat.

'My name is Frost,' he said.

Think It Over

1 Who was looking into a crystal ball?
2 Who was listening to her?
3 What prophecy was made about that woman's son?
4 Where was Mrs Watson's son?
5 What card did the fortune teller turn up for herself when Mrs Watson had gone?
6 How had Mrs Marsh shown that she had been impressed by Madame Clara's fortune telling?
7 Who was in the photograph that Madame Clara had knocked down?
8 What warning had that old lady given Madame Clara?
9 What numbers did the fortune teller see when she told her own fortune? What else did she see?
10 What did the fortune teller do on Tuesday 26th May?
11 Where did she go on the day after that and what did she do?
12 What happened to her?

Think It Out

1. Why might Madame Clara have taken her time about answering Mrs Watson's questions and 'let the suspense build up'?
2. When do you first learn that Mrs Watson's son might be a soldier?
3. Why do you think that Madame Clara changed from the crystal ball to cards to tell another part of Mrs Watson's fortune?
4. What shows that Mrs Watson is overjoyed to hear that her son is coming home?
5. How had Madame Clara guessed that Mrs Watson's son was a soldier?
6. How do you know that Madame Clara had not thought about Granny Lee for a long time? Why was finding the photograph on that particular day important?
7. In what way was Madame Clara's gift of real second sight not very helpful in telling fortunes for money?
8. What is the meaning of the ace of spades card when a fortune is told?
9. Why was the sight of an ice-cream seller frightening to Madame Clara?
10. How might the weather on the day she went into Swanton have reassured her?
11. What warning had the crystal ball given her about the van driver?

Using Words

1. 'Madame Clara closed her eyes as if what she had done had exhausted her powers.'
   Complete the sentences below with a few words of your own.
   She stared at me as if . . .
   The tree creaked and groaned in the wind as if . . .
   He ran home as if . . .
2. The first and last letters of three words near the beginning of the story are given on the next page. The words written in full on the left are almost opposite in meaning to each one. Find the words and use each in a sentence of your own.

39

glanced	g ... d
shouted	w .... d
jumble	s ...... e

3 What is the meaning of 'mumbo-jumbo'?
4 'She spent most of her time wandering apprehensively from room to room.' How did she feel?

Discuss Now

How do you feel about horoscopes, fortune tellers and things which claim to predict the future? Have you or anyone you know had a fortune told that came true? Or is it all nonsense? Or are horoscopes and fortune tellings so vague that you can't really tell whether they have come true or not? (You might discuss this point better if you could bring newspaper or magazine horoscopes into class.)

Write Now

1. How does it feel to be a young soldier who is part of a peace-keeping mission in Northern Ireland, or anywhere else in the world? Write a letter as a soldier to a close and sympathetic friend, describing what you have to do and how you feel about it.
2. Write the news item describing the fatal accident that happened to Madame Clara. You will have to decide whether Madame Clara is her real name and make up a full name (first and second names) for her. Give your news item a headline.
3. Write your own story about a fortune teller or about a horoscope. It could be a real story from your own experience or one you make up.

The Devil

In the long school holidays Simon stayed with Aunt Mildred and Uncle Piers; his mother died when he was two and his father sent him to boarding school when he was five. Simon's father was an engineer in Saudi Arabia, and he had only seen him twice in the last year.

Simon didn't mind this too much. Aunt Mildred had a large rambling house and 50 acres of land in the country; she owned a riding stables. Simon soon learnt to ride and by the time he was seven he was expert enough to help with the teaching of some of the younger children.

The rest of the time Simon spent exploring *Leesways*, as Aunt Mildred's house was called. It was a dark house, even in the middle of summer, with small windows and long, musty corridors.

A week before Simon's 8th birthday, Mrs Durance, Aunt Mildred's housekeeper, said she would give him anything he wanted for his birthday, provided it did not cost more than £5.

'You promise?' said Simon.

'As long as it . . .'

'It won't cost a penny,' said Simon.

'Well, you can have something extra in that case,' laughed Mrs Durance.

Mrs Durance was in a rare good mood because her back pain had receded for a few days.

'Let me in the room,' said Simon.

'What room?'

'You know.'

'Certainly not. Your aunt would have a fit.'

'You promised.'

'I said I'd buy you something, that's all.'

'You said you would give me anything I wanted under £5, and if you break your promise you will go to hell.'

'I'll go to hell if I let you in that room,' said Mrs Durance. She had put on the stern expression that usually meant her back was playing her up.

Of course, the fact that Mrs Durance would even break a promise to keep him out of the room, made Simon even more anxious to get in. The room was on the ground floor next to the kitchen. The door was permanently locked. The room was large, about 20 feet by 20, Simon guessed. His guess had to be based on measurements he'd made by adding together the area of all the other rooms and taking them away from the area of the whole of the ground floor, measured from outside. Simon was a careful boy; he'd even allowed for the two feet thickness of the walls in his calculations.

'I've seen in through the cracks in the windows,' said Simon.

He knew that all the windows were boarded up so tightly that not a chink of light showed through; he wanted to find out if Mrs Durance knew this as well.

'You've seen what's in there, then,' she laughed.

She knew! This meant she probably kept checking. If she kept checking that the boards or the iron bars that protected them hadn't rotted it must mean there was something really important in there.

He suddenly felt angry with Mrs Durance. She'd broken her promise and now she was laughing because she thought she'd outsmarted him.

'Tell me what's in there!' shouted Simon.

'The Devil,' said Mrs Durance.

'Don't be stupid. I'm nearly eight. Do you think I'll believe that rubbish?'

'There's a devil in there,' said Mrs Durance. 'Your Uncle locked him in there 8 years ago.'

Uncle Piers came home after Simon was in bed most nights. At weekends he sometimes played cards or draughts with Simon, but usually he sat reading papers and smoking a pipe.

'How could Uncle Piers catch a devil? He can't even catch Marmalade to throw him out at night.'

Marmalade was Aunt Milly's fat, ginger cat, Simon's friend or enemy, depending on the game they were playing.

'Your aunt and uncle wrestled with him and overpowered him together. They locked him in and my job is to see that he stays there. I have the only key. Now that's as much as I'm ever going to tell you, so forget it and decide on a present.'

'What's he look like?'

'Who?'

'The Devil.'

'Horns, a green tail and flaming red eyes. Now shut up.'

And Mrs Durance wouldn't say another word, despite Simon's pleas and threats.

It took Simon 3 days to undo one of the iron bars that protected the shuttering on the window that was out of the sight of anyone except other children coming up the driveway for their lessons.

Simon worked determinedly with a chisel and hammer he had stolen from Uncle Piers' garden shed; he set himself to work an hour a day, an hour when there were no pupils due and when Mrs Durance had gone to the village shop.

The bar gave suddenly; without warning it fell with a clatter. The boards were easier, but he still had to be careful not to smash them. Everything had to look normal in case Mrs Durance made an inspection.

The stale air seemed to rush out as the first board gave way; a dank, mouldy smell that made Simon wonder if the Devil had died and his body was still rotting.

Still there was no way in, even if Simon had dared to go. No way in for a boy that is, but a cat, even a fat cat, was a different matter. He'd use Marmalade to check the Devil story. If Marmalade came back alive, there was no green and blue devil.

Marmalade at first thought it was a new game, but as Simon had to squeeze him to get him between the bars he turned spiteful and bit him.

'I hope the Devil eats you, you horrible cat,' he said as he gave him a vicious push that sent him into the stale blackness.

Simon popped the boards back into position and went to look at the horses. He would give the Devil half an hour to devour Marmalade. That should be long enough; it was also safe, because Mrs Durance would not be back for at least 40 minutes.

As soon as Simon removed the boards Marmalade bounded out; there was certainly no need to rattle the cat biscuits. Marmalade had turned almost black. He was covered in grime and cobwebs. He spat and growled and the fur on his back was standing straight and stiff. Simon grabbed him with the gardening gloves he'd worn for the purpose and dunked him in the kitchen sink; a filthy cat might have given Mrs Durance a clue.

Marmalade was clearly frightened and full of hate, but he definitely wasn't dead. Whatever was in there, it wasn't a live devil. Marmalade had cleared the way for Simon's entry.

This had to be with Mrs Durance's key. He'd already found out that the keys were kept in her handbag and wherever Mrs Durance went, her handbag went as well, or rather it had done in the 3 days that Simon had been watching her closely.

Simon's chance came on Saturday morning. Uncle Piers had gone for a walk, Aunt Mildred was with a pupil and Mrs Durance had gone to pay the milkman, with the purse that was used for the housekeeping money; she left her handbag on the dining-room sideboard.

Mrs Durance and the milkman always had a chat, a 10-minute chat at least, thought Simon as he rifled through the handbag. There were at least a dozen keys on the ring. Even in his fear Simon remained methodical; he tried the biggest key first and worked clockwise round the ring, so that he wouldn't waste time trying some keys twice.

The 8th key turned slowly but surely in the lock. Simon quickly re-locked the door and carefully prised the key off the ring. The rest of the bunch were at the bottom of Mrs Durance's bag well before she'd finished gossiping with the milkman.

The next day was Wednesday. Every Wednesday Mrs Durance went to do 'the big shop', as she called it. She would be out for at least 2 hours; Aunt Milly had pupils for both the hours (Simon had checked in the book) and Uncle Piers was away for the week.

At 11.15 Simon turned the key and at last entered the room that had obsessed him for the past month. He carried a torch and a fat hawthorn stick, the stick to beat off anything alive and nasty such as a rat – he did not believe the Devil story, especially as Marmalade had emerged unscathed.

Simon closed the door carefully behind him and, his heart beating violently, began to shine the torch around the room.

For 5 minutes he remained motionless except for the movement of his arm as he played the powerful beam of Uncle Piers' torch around the objects in the room. Gradually his heartbeat returned to normal, then

45

suddenly raced again in anger instead of fear. He had been fooled by Mrs Durance – the room was full of old junk, no devil, no dead bodies, no caskets of jewels, not the smallest sign of any of the things he'd spent the last 2 days imagining he might find.

An old bike, a table-lamp, a chest of drawers and some crates of bottles were the only unbroken things in sight. There were broken chairs, a bed without legs, some fractured golf clubs and a pile of splintered planks.

In his rage and disappointment Simon ransacked the place like a demented burglar; he pulled the drawers from the chest (they contained a few nails and screws) and threw them to the floor. He kicked the lamp against the wall and knocked over the crates of bottles. Some of the bottles were full; two smashed and the pale liquid spread over the filthy floor. It tasted horrible and set off a mini-fire in his stomach. He threw it against the wall, and left the room in a rage, forgetting even to lock the door.

Three days later Simon had almost forgotten his disappointment. He had a new project, to persuade Aunt Milly to let him ride Comus, a big stallion who was reserved for expert adult riders. The best he had achieved so far was a vague promise that she 'would see' in the next summer holidays. Simon was thinking out the next stage in his Comus campaign when there was a knock on his bedroom door. Uncle Piers came in and sat solemnly on the wicker armchair next to Simon's bed.

'I think I'm too sleepy to play draughts,' said Simon.

'I want to ask you something, Simon,' said Uncle Piers.

Simon looked at his thin, lined face; he knew instinctively it must be something about the room.

'Have you ever been in the room next to the dining-room?'

Uncle Piers' brown eyes studied Simon's face.

'Well, of course I have, Uncle.'

'When?' said Uncle Piers, sharply.

'Well, every day. I've just been there to fetch my glass of water.'

'I don't mean the kitchen, Simon. I mean the room that's next to the kitchen.'

'There isn't a room next to the kitchen, is there Uncle? There's just the false door that Mrs Durance told me about.'

'What did she say?'

Simon screwed up his face, pretending to search his memory.

'Well, one day I just asked what was behind the door; Mrs Durance said it was just a false door. Is there a room there Uncle?'

'No, Simon. It's just a false door as Mrs Durance says. I'm sorry I troubled you. Now go to sleep.'

Simon waited 2 days before he asked Aunt Milly the obvious question.

'Has Mrs Durance gone to see her mother again, Aunt? She forgot to say goodbye.'

'Yes, Simon. Her mother's very ill. She will have to stay quite a long time. Uncle Piers has advertised for another housekeeper until Mrs Durance can come back. It won't be until after you've gone to school.'

Simon spent the day brooding. He was certain of two things; Uncle Piers had sacked Mrs Durance and Aunt Milly was very upset. Both things were connected with the room; when he remembered he'd forgotten to lock it, he found someone else had already done so. That someone else must have been Uncle Piers. So Uncle Piers had a key; but so had Simon, and Uncle Piers thought the second key had gone off with Mrs Durance. He probably wouldn't change the lock; Simon had an idea that might work.

'I've had a really nice birthday,' said Simon. 'Thank you very much, Aunt Milly.'

Aunt Milly looked up from the table, where she was writing her pupils' bills.

'Well, I'm so pleased. We've enjoyed having you. It's school again in a week, but the time will soon pass. You'll be back for Christmas.'

'I've brought you a present for being so nice to me,' said Simon. He pulled out a bottle of drink he'd hidden under his chair.

'Where did you get that?' said Aunt Milly sharply.

Simon pretended to look guilty.

'It was one of Mrs Durance's bottles. She used to drink them when we were on our own. She left some behind in her hidey-hole and I thought she wouldn't miss just one . . . that's not really stealing, is it Aunt?'

Aunt Mildred followed Simon to the kitchen. He bent under the sink and pointed to a shelf at the top of the waste pipe. Aunt Milly reached in and pulled out one after another the six bottles of vodka that Simon had removed from the room and stored there at dinner-time.

Simon had never seen Aunt Milly so agitated. Her hands were shaking and her face was pale.

'I'm sorry if I've upset you; I didn't think it was really stealing and I wanted to give you something,' said Simon, studying his Aunt's face closely.

'Oh, it's not your fault, dear. It was a kind thought. It's just that Uncle Piers would be very upset if he knew that Mrs Durance had been hiding drink in the house. You see, Uncle Piers is very much against alcohol . . . very much against it,' Aunt Milly said staring vacantly out of the window.

'We'd better get rid of it, then?' said Simon.

'I'll see to it,' said Aunt Milly. 'Now you'd better be off to bed; you may be a grown-up boy now, but you still need a full 8 hours sleep.'

Simon went obediently to bed. Just before he went to sleep Aunt Milly came to kiss him goodnight.

'I think the bottles Mrs Durance brought should be our little secret,' she said. 'Uncle Piers would be very upset if he knew; you wouldn't want Uncle Piers upset, would you dear?'

'No Aunt,' said Simon, as she bent to kiss him. 'I promise I won't tell Uncle Piers.'

Simon settled down snugly in his bed; he had smelt the vodka on Aunt Milly's breath. It seemed his hunch had been right.

Two days later Simon fell off Comus; he wasn't hurt, but Aunt Milly was cross.

'I knew I shouldn't have let you; you're far too young,' she said.

'Alright, Aunt,' said Simon.

He waited for 2 days and then asked Aunt Milly why the bottles were still hidden under the sink. Then he asked her if he could try Comus again; she agreed. Later that morning Simon fetched three more bottles from the room to replace the ones that had gone missing. Aunt Milly didn't seem to notice.

Simon's last few days before returning to school were happy ones; he had achieved every small boy's ambition. He could do what he wished; he rode Comus, even when an important customer wanted him; he stayed up as late as he wished; he was allowed to go to the village by himself and buy whatever he wanted.

But Simon was the only happy one in the house. Most nights he drifted into sleep with the distant sound of the raised and angry voices of his Aunt and Uncle in his ears. Sometimes he heard the sound of breaking glass or crying.

Aunt Milly grew daily more forgetful and vague. She forgot appointments, shouted at the customers, and one day even fell off her horse. Simon grew worried, and decided to bring the bottles from the room singly. It seemed to make little difference. Aunt Milly made more frequent trips to town, returning with suspicious-looking boxes.

Aunt Milly was tearful as she waved goodbye to Simon at the station. Uncle Piers wore the grim expression he had had continuously for the last fortnight. In a way Simon was glad to escape; he realised his freedom to do what he wished would have soon come to an end anyway, and he had five £1 coins in his pockets – Aunt Milly's final bribe.

Two days before the Christmas holidays Simon had an unexpected visitor – his father.

'How do you fancy spending a warm Christmas in Saudi Arabia?' he asked.

'I don't mind,' said Simon, 'but I think I'd sooner stay with Aunt Milly.'

'I'm afraid that's out, Simon. Aunt Milly's not well.'

'Has she had an accident?'

'Well, not exactly an accident. You see, Simon . . .'

His father hesitated but then went on to explain that Aunt Milly had once been what was called an alcoholic. Simon, of course, was far too young to understand what this meant but, his father explained, it was like a disease. Ten years ago Aunt Milly, with Uncle Piers' help, had managed to cure herself. Now, for some reason, she'd suddenly lapsed again.

'I suppose she'll soon be better again,' said Simon.

'Well, I'd like to think so, but I'm afraid I doubt it. She's had to go into a home, Simon. She's very ill.'

'Maybe I could help with the riding school,' said Simon.

'There isn't one now,' said his father sadly. 'There's been a lot of trouble; it's had to close.'

Simon looked so upset that his father regretted going into the details; a boy of eight was far too young to understand.

'I know you'll miss Aunt and Uncle and the riding school. But I promise you, you can have riding lessons where we are going.'

'I'd like a horse of my own,' said Simon.

'We'll see,' said his father. Simon knew that meant he'd get one.

There were times in the last two days at school that Simon felt vaguely sorry for Aunt Milly, Uncle Piers and even Mrs Durance. But he soon realised such feelings were foolish, particularly for Mrs Durance. It was all her stupid fault for saying there was a devil in the room.

Think It Over

1. Why did Simon stay with Aunt Mildred during the school holidays?
2. Where was 'the room'?
3. What did Mrs Durance say was in the room?
4. Who had the key to the room?
5. How did Simon use Marmalade the cat?
6. How did Simon find the right key?
7. What did Simon take in the room and why?
8. Why was Simon so angry?
9. What was Simon's new project?
10. Who else had a key to the room?
11. How did Simon bribe Aunt Milly?
12. Why did Aunt Milly and Uncle Piers quarrel at night?
13. Why did Aunt Milly have to go into a home?

Think It Out

1. Why did Simon want to go to the room so much?
2. Why might there have been alcohol in the room?
3. How did we know Mrs Durance knew about Aunt Milly's illness?
4. Why was Simon not suspected by Uncle Piers?
5. In what ways was Simon spoiled in the story?
6. 'If there is any devil in the story, it is in Simon'. Explain this statement.

Using Words

1 Use each of these words in sentences of your own in two different ways: stable; fit; board; draughts; pop; lock.
2 Look up these words in a dictionary and write down their meaning: recede; methodical; obsessed; unscathed; vague.
3 What describing words are used about the room and the things in it. Make a list.
4 What is the difference between 'prise' and 'prize'?

Discuss Now

What are the problems associated with alcohol? Why do young people want to drink? How might we drink less as a nation?
Should young children always be told the truth about things? Can you think of any instances when it would be unwise?

Write Now

1 Write a character study of Simon from the things you learn about him in the story.
2 Describe a room or shed full of junk.
3 You have to film this story for TV. Write down actors and actresses who could play the four main characters. If you don't know their names put down the series they appear in and the part they play in it. Give reasons for your choices. Then make a list of the properties you need for the room.

The Red-eyed Cats

Mrs Kentucket chose us: we didn't choose her. We were having tea one day when she knocked on the door. I went. A small lady with almost the suggestion of a humped-back stood there. Though there were no lines on her face she looked old. She was dressed in a red headscarf over long black hair and she wore a black cloak that came almost to her ankles.

'Is your mother in, dearie?' Her voice sounded like a rasp on wood.

'Yes,' I said.

'Get her then please, my pretty.'

I went and got mother. 'Oh, what is it, Deborah? Can't you send them away at teatime. My digestion.'

'She wants you.'

'Who is it?'

'Never seen her before.'

'Selling something I'll be bound. You go Peter.'

'No,' said Dad, weakly. 'She wants you.'

My mother got up, sighing.

A few moments later she returned smiling. The woman was with her.

'You know I've been looking for a cleaning lady. Well, Mrs Kentucket is looking for work.'

'Splendid,' said my father and went back to his tea. 'Arrange whatever you like, Joan.'

You could see he thought the woman odd but he knew how my mother had been on and on about a cleaner. So it was arranged that Mrs Kentucket would come three mornings a week.

53

She cleaned well and quickly and my mother was highly pleased. On the rare occasions I came into contact with her I found it difficult to look her in the face. Her eyes seemed to burn right through you. So I kept out of her way. She always hummed a tune when she worked which I could even hear in my room when she was downstairs. It was always the same tune; not a pop number but a sort of chant. It added to her weirdness.

It was in the third week that the cat appeared. A large black sculptured cat with red eyes was on the mantlepiece.

'Is it yours?' asked my mother.

'No.'

'I thought you'd made it at school.'

'I'm not that good at art.'

'Must be something to do with your father. I do hope it is not one of his silly presents. I think it's hideous.'

But Dad denied all knowledge of the cat. So Mum asked Mrs Kentucket if she knew anything about it.

'I meant to ask you if I could leave it here. I've three unruly children staying with me and, as it's a family heirloom, I'd be much obliged if you could look after it. They could break it. And I've two more. It's one of a set. Could I leave them, please, as well.' It was a strange request but my mother did not want to upset a good cleaner.

The next day one appeared on the chest-of-drawers in my bedroom and the other in my parents' bedroom.

'They can't be all in the same room,' was all Mrs Kentucket would say. That night I awoke slowly fighting for consciousness. Moonlight slanted across the bed from a slit in the curtains. I pulled myself up on an elbow.

The red eyes were staring at me from across the room. Penetratingly red, they bore into mine like laser beams. Whichever way I turned my head I could still see the eyes, as if reflected in the back of mine. Even if I buried my head in the pillow my own eyeballs seemed lit up with redness. My head sung with a vibrating muzziness. Was I ill? Was it a feverish nightmare? I pinched myself. It was no dream and I was not hot or sweating.

A chanting noise played on a low-pitched wind instrument slowly came into my consciousness. Voices hummed with it. I gradually realized it was the tune Mrs Kentucket hummed during the day.

People were downstairs in our house! I had to get up and warn my parents. But the muzziness controlled my body. The sheets seemed wrapped round me like clinging mud.

The next thing it was morning. I sat up and looked at the cat. There it was harmlessly on the chest-of-drawers. Its eyes did not shine. I must have dreamed it. My mother also said nothing about strange happenings in the night, so it must have been a nightmare. Except that it did not explain the strange incense-like smell downstairs which my mother and father could not detect, having poor senses of smell. When I mentioned it my mother said it must have been the curry we had the night before.

I also had a feeling that the furniture was not quite as we had left it. I examined the cat on the mantlepiece. It was quite innocuous.

That night I turned the cat's eyes to the wall. Surprisingly I went to sleep quickly. But I awoke with a start and sat up. The red eyes of the cat held me. They were reflected onto the wall, onto my dressing-table mirror and into my eyes. The muzziness made me feel heavy in every limb. From below came the strange instrument and the chanting. This was really happening! I must get out of bed and warn my parents! But I could not move from the bed.

Suddenly there was a snarling. My heart palpitated. Then I realized it was my cat. She was sitting spitting at the red-eyed cat. I could see her vaguely through the redness in my eyeballs. Then she sprang. There was a crash as the sculptured cat fell on the floor. It smashed to pieces and the red eyes rolled about like marbles. As they rolled their light gradually diminished.

I could now see properly and there was no muzziness controlling me. I wanted to hug my cat but she had leapt out of the open window at the crash onto the kitchen roof.

I crept to my parents' room. On the landing the chanting sounded much louder. Then I stopped. In my parents' room was another cat. It could control me as soon as I opened the door. I crept down the stairs.

Between the lounge and the kitchen there was a service hatch. I peered through the slit. The smell of incense was strong. I saw Mrs Kentucket in a black robe sitting in an armchair which was raised up on our settee. All the furniture in the room was turned to face the north window. Two men and two women were sitting cross-legged on the floor swaying from side to side as they chanted. They seemed to be in a hypnotic state. The red eyes of the cat were reflected in Mrs Kentucket's. I sweated in my nightdress. I must go to my parents. A man was standing on the stairs.

I turned and ran out of the kitchen door which was open and into the small coppice that surrounds our house. I confused my own laboured breathing with someone following me. Brambles scratched my face; my nightdress was torn; my bare feet ached. Our nearest neighbours were half a mile away. Would I reach them or would my body be found in the wood the following morning?

I did reach them and hammered on their door and cried out till they came. Seeing me in a torn nightdress and bleeding they rang the police.

The police came to the neighbour's house with my father and distraught mother. They listened patiently as

I blurted out my story. My mother explained that I must have been sleep-walking. Mrs Kentucket was not in the house; nor were any other people. I went on and on about the cats. My mother explained that I must have knocked the one over in my room when I was sleepwalking. It was the age I was at.

I begged the police to question Mrs Kentucket and to examine the cats. They humoured me and said they would but I know nothing was done.

Next day Mrs Kentucket removed the cats at my mother's request. But she also handed in her notice. I have been made to go away on holiday. I do not know what is worse: not being believed or fearing that in some dark place some red eyes will stare into mine and once more I will be under the control of Mrs Kentucket. I can still smell something in our house but I have said nothing to my parents as I know my father is considering calling in a psychiatrist.

Think It Over

1. What descriptive details were given about Mrs Kentucket?
2. Why did Deborah's mother not want to answer the door?
3. What was Mrs Kentucket employed as?
4. What did Mrs Kentucket do while she worked?
5. What appeared in the third week of her employment?
6. Why did Deborah's Mum let Mrs Kentucket bring the cats?
7. How did Deborah feel when she woke up?
8. What noise did she hear?
9. What was the smell downstairs?
10. How did Deborah's cat react to the red-eyed cat?
11. What did Deborah see downstairs?
12. Why could Deborah not get back up the stairs?
13. What did she do when she couldn't?
14. How did we know at the end of the story that they do not believe Deborah?

Think It Out

1. Why might Deborah's Mum have employed Mrs Kentucket although she looked odd?
2. What interest did her father take in the running of the house?
3. What is devilish or witchlike about Mrs Kentucket?
4. Why might Mrs Kentucket have wanted to use the house?
5. Why was Deborah not believed?
6. How might it affect her future?

Using Words

1. Write down one unusual surname you have heard.
2. Do you know what your surname means or where it comes from?
3. *Headscarf*. What other words do you know beginning 'head'? Make a list.
4. What words would you use to describe a laser beam?

Discuss Now

When have you not been believed about something that happened to you?
Is there any evidence you have heard about or read about to support modern-day witchcraft? Were there witches in the past or were some old ladies treated cruelly? Should young children read about witches today?

Write Now

1. From the few hints given write a short character description of Deborah's mother.
2. Describe how you would have felt in Deborah's situation:
    (a) as you crept down the stairs and saw what was happening;
    (b) afterwards if you are not believed.
3. Deborah's story is believed by a local newspaper reporter. Write her report and headline.

The Expanding Man

I got on the train at Tadworth. I was journeying to Fording, some 20 minutes down the line. It was a hot June afternoon. The train, as it pulled in, had few passengers. The coach I got in seemed empty. I picked a middle compartment and settled down to read my *Daily Mail*. No one else boarded the train.

The guard blew his whistle and the train was just about to pull out when a fat man came running on to the platform. He was dressed in a white suit. He was bald and the top of his head had brown marks like coffee stains. I could see he was breathing heavily and was probably not used to such exertion. Mine was the nearest compartment; he made for it, opened the door, and flung himself in as the train moved off. He said nothing as he tripped over my legs and flopped, like a shuddering jelly, into the far corner of the seat opposite. His breath came like a rapidly switched on and off vacuum cleaner. His red neck bulged over his collar and I remember thinking how ludicrous it was for him to wear a tie on a day like this.

He was not a man you would have missed in a crowd and here, in this closed compartment my eyes were drawn to him rather than the paper I was pretending to read.

The train was uncommonly hot even for the time of day and I had the suspicion that the temperature had risen several degrees since his entrance. I wondered briefly whether to pull down the blind, but the sun was coming from his side of the train.

His breath was now coming more easily, if you can ever describe a smoker's breath in that way, for I could see three heavily-stained, nicotined fingers on his right ringed hand, and he also exuded a smell of tobacco.

I wondered whether to speak about the blind and make a casual remark about the weather, but he did not look at me, staring straight ahead. The train now picked up speed which normally induced a feeling of relaxation and I gazed out of the window at the rising and dipping telephone wires. But not this afternoon; my body felt tense since his arrival and my paper rustled as I fumbled to turn its pages, not being able to concentrate on any section for more than a few seconds. There was something about this man, apart from his extreme fatness, which was not normal. I took a quick glance at my watch. I still had 17 minutes of his company before I could alight at Fording.

He was perspiring freely and he mopped his bald head with a red-spotted handkerchief, flattening the few greasy black hairs. His white suit showed patches of sweat under the arms and he put his nicotined finger inside his shirt collar as if to let some air in.

It was at that moment that his neck appeared to flow out of his collar; a mass of bulging, black-stubbled flesh. It was like one of those surgical collars people wear only this was of quivering skin. I dropped my paper and fumbled to pick it up. As I did so I could see that his neck was even bigger now oozing out over his shoulders like a red mould.

I rubbed my eyes, thinking they were affected by the heat. When I stopped I still saw the same horrific sight. I half rose to escape out of the door to the corridor but at that moment his arm and hand shot across it, pouring out of his jacket like liquid rubber. The hand itself must have been a foot across with blubbery fingers on the end. I tried to cry out but no sound came from my dry throat and the only scream was in the tunnel of my mind. The left side of his body now bulged out like a giant balloon along the seat opposite. His head got bigger by the second, looking like a latex puppet on a TV show. Each line on his face was an oily rivulet of sweat; each pimple was wart-like and as big as a 2p-piece. The heat that came from this mass was like a many-barred electric fire. His knees then blew up to the size of footballs and became wedged against my seat.

My greatest fear was of fainting. My only escape was out of the outside door, so much flesh barred the way to the inner one. But that meant certain death as the train was at full speed. The communication cord was on his side. I would have to climb over flesh to reach it. I stared out of the window, wresting my gaze from his body for the moment as if expecting help to flow by outside. The banks of the trackside rose steeply, denoting we were approaching Attercliffe Tunnel.

With a whoosh we were in it. To my horror no lights came on. What if I should feel his body touching mine in the echoing darkness? I could feel my heart beating against the back of the seat as I shrunk into it. I knew I would surely faint if I did. And in that faint I would be crushed against the window by his expanding, rubbery body. My only hope was that Fording lay just beyond the tunnel.

I put my head between my knees and prayed. I knew I dare not look up even if I survived to the end of the tunnel.

The train slowed. Was it going to stop in the tunnel or had we reached Fording? His breathing grew to a crescendo of wheezing. At any moment his flesh would reach mine. His heat was radiated to the core of my body.

Then daylight filtered through my closed eyelids. The train came to a halt. I fumbled with the handle of the door. My fingers touched flesh. It was like hot fish-skin, but I knew I must get out whether we were by the platform or not. I jumped.

I found myself not on the platform at Fording but on the platform at Tadworth. I took in the familiar surroundings. Yes, there was the ticket-office. And there was the waiting-room. There was no doubt it was Tadworth. My rapidly beating heart slowed. There was no train in the station. I had never made the journey that had given me such a nightmare.

Then the lines hummed. The train for Fording was approaching. I knew nothing would get me on that train. But I still waited till it drew into the station. The reflecting windows surged by me. I was facing an empty coach and compartment.

I turned and ran past the ticket-office and down the stairs. As I did so a man in a white suit passed me running up. He was red-faced, fat and bald and there were brown spots on his head. He mopped himself with a red-spotted handkerchief as he ran.

Think It Over

1. Where was the traveller going?
2. How many people boarded the train?
3. Why did the fat man breathe so heavily?
4. How was his breathing described?
5. What normally soothed the traveller as the train picked up speed?
6. Why was the traveller not relaxed that day?
7. Which part of the fat man's body expanded first?
8. Why couldn't the traveller leave the compartment?
9. What was the traveller's greatest fear?
10. What showed that the train was approaching a tunnel?
11. Where was the traveller at the end of the story?

Think It Out

1. What kind of a train coach was it?

2 Why did the traveller want to keep looking at the fat man?
3 Why did the traveller fumble with the pages of his newspaper?
4 How does the writer convey the impression of extreme heat in the story?
5 What is the most horrific part of the story?
6 What did you expect to happen in the tunnel?
7 Have you any explanation for the ending of the story?

Using Words

1 'His breath came like a rapidly switched on and off vacuum cleaner'. In what other ways could you describe heavy breathing?
2 Use 'exuded' and 'crescendo' in sentences of your own.
3 When might you use 'alight' and when 'get off'?
4 What words are used in the passage to suggest unpleasant expansion?

Discuss Now

1 Why do people tend to be reserved and not talk to each other in trains in this country? Should people talk more?
2 What is your most frightening experience or dream that seemed real?
3 What kind of people open up conversations on trains? In groups act out a scene in a railway carriage where one person tries to draw others into a conversation.

Write Now

1 Describe what it is like to be on a busy station platform.
2 Using some of the words from the story describe what it is like to travel by train or bus on a very hot day.
3 You are travelling on a familiar train journey. Suddenly the view from the window is completely strange and unworldly. What is the explanation. Write your story.

The Strange Case of Mrs Harris

A nurse opened the glass door and the by now large gathering of visitors moved through. It was like a race, thought Karen, where some of the competitors weren't trying. Within 20 metres the leaders, mostly those clutching boxes of chocolates or flowers, were clicking their way down the long marble corridor, well in front of those walking slowly, looking nervous or solemn.

Karen decided it depended on who you were visiting and how ill they were. Grandad was very ill; he'd been unconscious for 3 days and was in a little room by himself, in what her mum had called 'intensive care'. Despite her Mum's warning Grandad was still a shock. He lay on his back, his wrinkled old face propped up by two pillows. There were tubes in his nose and tubes strapped to his arms; the tubes led to hanging bottles; there were various charts and diagrams clipped to the bottom of his bed.

Karen's first shock reaction was that he must have died and they were using him for some horrible experiment; then she noticed his bumpy chest rising and falling, but with long pauses in between. Karen tried not to look at the bottles and tubes; she noticed the grey hairs on his chest; they were thicker and longer than those left on his nearly bald head.

'Karen's come today, Dad,' said Mum, speaking slowly with her face near Grandad's ear.

For the next 10 minutes Karen's Mum told Grandad all the news. It was plain he didn't hear a single word. Karen grew more uneasy and embarrassed.

'He can't hear you, Mum,' she said.
'You never know,' said her Mum. 'You tell him something.'
Karen was tongue-tied with fright.
'Hello, Grandad,' she said eventually.
'Do you see 'em?' said Grandad, pointing a hand to the ceiling.
Karen's Mum made a choking noise and Karen's legs began to shake. She reached for and held her Mum's hand.
'There they go,' shouted Grandad, struggling to sit up and pointing again.
'Who goes where, Dad?' said Karen's Mum.
'Do you see 'em?' shouted Grandad.

It was plain that Grandad was still unconscious, but his ramblings were the first step to his recovery. Within a week he was sitting up without his tubes; within 10 days he was poddling around the hospital. Within a fortnight he was nearly back to normal – mischievous and awkward as ever. For instance it was a mistake telling him what he said when he was unconscious. The day after, Aunt Irene came to visit him; Grandad didn't like her; he lay on his back with his eyes shut.

'Irene's come, Dad,' said Karen's Mum.
'I seem 'em,' shouted Grandad. 'The big 'un is a purple one with a nose like a clothes peg.'
Aunt Irene's face went the colour of her new mauve dress. Her visit lasted 3 minutes. She rushed out dabbing her long nose with a handkerchief. Grandad lapsed back 'unconscious', a smile of satisfaction on his face.
'That was an awful thing to do, Dad,' said Karen's Mum.
Grandad gave a big snore and pretended to wake up.
'Oh, hello,' he said. 'I've been unconscious again.'

But Grandad's tricks were nothing compared to his

awkwardness. He wasn't going to live with anybody; he was going to stay by himself in his cottage; he'd looked after himself for 10 years and didn't see any reason why he couldn't now.

'But the doctor says you could have another attack any time,' Karen's Mum argued.

'And your cottage is miles from anywhere,' said Karen.

'Miles – rubbish,' said Grandad. 'It's a 100 yards from old Simey's.'

'But he's deaf; he wouldn't hear you shouting.'

'I wouldn't shout if I was unconscious,' said Grandad.

Grandad won, as usual, except that he reluctantly agreed to have a housekeeper.

'She can keep well out of my road,' said Grandad.

'She can have the two rooms at the back,' said Karen's Mum.

'Why can't she live in the cellar?' said Grandad.

'Don't be ridiculous; you've got enough rooms to house half a dozen housekeepers.'

'I want a young, good-looking one,' said Grandad. 'I don't want anything with a boat-race like our Irene's.'

But the only person to answer the advert was Mrs Harris. She was rather a shock.

'I come about looking after the old gentleman,' said Mrs Harris in a voice like a billygoat. Karen had to repress a giggle. Mrs Harris had a white square face surmounted by an enormous bouquet of ginger hair. She wore a long, green skirt with black lace-up boots.

'Oh, yes, come in,' said Karen.

It took 6 days to persuade Grandad to let Mrs Harris in to his house.

'She's as ugly as an old boot,' said Grandad.

'That doesn't matter. She's well-meaning and kindly,' said Karen's Mum.

'She wears a ginger wig,' said Grandad.

'Yes, I think she does,' said Karen's Mum. 'But lots of

ladies do if their hair's thinning. I know it looks silly, but it doesn't matter what she looks like. She'll look after you well, that's the main thing.'

Of course, there was bound to be a settling-in period, and everybody expected Grandad to complain about poor old Mrs Harris. They weren't disappointed. At first he complained about her cooking.

'Columbus could make better chips than 'er,' he said.

'Who's Columbus?' said Karen.

'It's an old, mangy cat he used to have,' explained her Mum.

Then Grandad started accusing Mrs Harris of awful things.

'She goes out in the middle of the night. I reckon she's a prossytute.'

'A what?' said Karen.

'One of them women who sells themselves to men.'

Karen giggled all the way home. The idea of Mrs Harris being a 'prossytute' was as likely as Grandad winning the London marathon.

But he kept up his campaign. He accused Mrs Harris of having wild parties when he was trying to get to sleep, of trying to poison him by putting arsenic in his dinner and finally of singing filthy songs in the bathroom.

There was a meeting before the family set off for their fortnight in Spain. It was decided that as Grandad couldn't stand the sight of Aunt Irene, Mrs Harris would have to cope. Mum had a long talk with her.

'Well, I'll not deny he can be a cussed old genilman,' said Mrs Harris. 'But it's water off a duck's back to me. All old genilmen is cussed in their different ways. I looked after plenty. I'll manage him all right, missus.' This was easily the longest speech Mrs Harris had made in the 6 weeks she had been in charge of Grandad. Mum was re-assured.

'She's a rough old lady, but her heart's in the right

place,' she reported.

So off they all went to Torremolinos. It was a hot fortnight; they enjoyed themselves. Mum wrote three cards to Grandad.

When they arrived home there was a frightening note among the letters piled up behind the front door.

'Ring the hospital,' it said.

Dad, Mum and Karen set off immediately. The nurse looked accusingly at them.

'He's been here for 10 days. It was made clear to you before that he shouldn't be left on his own.'

'But he had a housekeeper,' said Mum, beginning to cry with guilt.

'There's been no sign of a housekeeper, or any other visitors,' said the nurse coldly.

'But who brought him in?'

'He collapsed in a shop in town. The shopkeeper rang for the ambulance.'

'Will he recover?' said Dad.

'You're lucky,' said the nurse. 'He's showing signs of coming out of it again.'

'Can we see him?'

The nurse led the way. She stopped in front of the door and hesitated.

'Was there anything . . . er . . . unusual about your father, Mrs Bond?'

'He was rather awkward,' said Mum hesitantly. 'What's he done?'

'Oh, he's done nothing,' said the nurse, 'but when he was brought in he was wearing rather peculiar clothes.'

The family watched in horrified silence as the nurse extracted a green skirt and a large red wig from a nearby cupboard.

'Oh, God, he's murdered Mrs Harris,' wailed Mum.

'And scalped her,' muttered Karen.

They scurried into Grandad's room. He lay peacefully

on his back; there were no tubes or bottles.
Mum sat by the bed and grasped his hand.

'Dad, Dad, can you hear me?'

'No,' whispered Grandad.

'What have you done with Mrs Harris?' said Mum.

Grandad began to snore gently.

'For heaven's sake! This is serious. Please tell us what you've done with Mrs Harris.'

'There weren't no Mrs Harris,' said Grandad.

'Is he rambling, or is he being awkward?' said Dad.

Suddenly Grandad opened his pale blue eyes; he took criticism from his daughter, but wasn't going to be accused of being awkward by her husband.

'Mrs Harris was a cat-burglar,' said Grandad.

'Don't be ridiculous, dear,' said Mum.

'She was also a fella,' said Grandad. 'And if you don't believe me go and ask her. I locked her in the cellar.'

Grandad slipped back into a genuine state of unconsciousness. The family looked at each other in horror.

'Can he be telling the truth?' said Dad.

'I'm sure he is,' said Mum.

Three hours later Carl Reynolds was carried on a stretcher from the deep, dank cellar of a country cottage to Grenton Hospital. Carl had spent his life in and out of prison; he had a collection of recent thefts hidden in the cellar. The police had always kept an eye on Carl; they'd been wondering for weeks where he had been hiding. Now they would never have to wonder again. 2 hours after he entered hospital he was taken to the mortuary.

It was too horrible to contemplate; Grandad, still slipping in and out of consciousness, had murdered him.

'It was manslaughter,' said Mum for the tenth time.

'Surely they won't do anything to Grandad,' said Karen.

'It served the man right in a way,' said Dad.

'He didn't deserve to die like that,' said Mum.

It was a month before the police were allowed to interview Grandad. Mum and the doctor were present.

'I want to ask you a few questions about the person you knew as Mrs Harris,' began the Sergeant.

'I never heard of a Mrs Harris,' said Grandad.

'The person who lived with you?'

'My wife's been dead 10 years,' said Grandad.

'Who do you live with?' said the Sergeant patiently.

'With my daughter. I've been there since I had my first attack,' said Grandad.

'That's not true, Dad,' said Mum, looking uneasily at the Sergeant.

'You're all ganging up against me,' said Grandad, and started to cry.

The doctor insisted that Grandad was left alone for a few more days. When the Sergeant returned he got the same story, this time with a long description of where he lived in his daughter's house and how he'd given up his cottage because he couldn't manage to look after himself any more.

'His mind's repressing the truth because it can't cope with it,' explained the doctor. 'That kind of amnesia is quite common. I don't see how you can possibly charge him. It would certainly kill him; he hasn't long to live anway.'

In the end the police closed the case. The inquest on Carl Reynolds returned a verdict of Death by Misadventure. Grandad came to live in the room he insisted he had been living in for the past 6 months.

A year later Grandad had his third heart attack. He was out shopping with Karen. Karen was at the sweet counter when she heard a faint whimper behind her. She turned to see Grandad on the floor. A woman with a mass of ginger hair was bending over him.

'I seemed to give him a shock,' the woman was saying

agitatedly. 'I just touched him on the shoulder to ask him to move aside. When he turned round he just dropped; we'd better get an ambulance, dear.'
Grandad died in the ambulance before it reached the hospital.

Think It Over

1. Why was Grandad in a little room by himself?
2. What did Karen's Mum do on the hospital visit?
3. How did Karen react to the visit?
4. What did Grandad do when Aunt Irene came?
5. What did Grandad want to do when he came out of hospital?
6. How did Mrs Harris speak?
7. How did Mum explain about Mrs Harris's wig?
8. What did Grandad accuse Mrs Harris of?
9. Where did Grandad have his second attack?
10. How was he dressed when brought to the hospital?
11. What was Mrs Harris and what did Grandad do to 'her'?
12. What happened when the police interviewed Grandad?
13. How did Grandad die?

Think It Out

1. Why did Mrs Harris apply for the job?
2. How might he/she have died?
3. Which of Grandad's accusations about 'her' might have been true?
4. Give some evidence of Grandad's awkwardness.
5. How did Grandad fool the police?
6. Why did Grandad have a third heart attack?

Using Words

1. Why is the word 'clicking' used in the first paragraph?
2. What does 'tongue-tied' mean? Also explain 'to get one's tongue around' and 'to have on the tip of one's tongue'.
3. 'Poddling' is a dialect word. What might it mean?
4. 'Boat-race' is Cockney rhyming slang. What does it mean? Give some other slang words for the same thing.

Discuss Now

Why do some old people want to live alone? Should they be allowed to? What are the advantages and disadvantages of living in an old people's home?
What confidence tricks have you heard of or read about?
This is a comic/sinister story. Films called 'Black Comedies' are very popular. What does the term mean? Discuss some real-life incidents that are both funny and frightening at the same time.

Write Now

1 Write a police report of either: How they found Carl Reynolds; the sergeant's interview with Grandad.
2 Write a newspaper report of the incident in three short paragraphs with a headline.
3 You are trapped in a damp cellar for a day. Write about your feelings and experience.

The Mask

It had been a dare really. Tom, being the smallest, had been able to get through the lavatory window at the back of The Fun Shop. The others stood in the yard keeping watch after pushing him through. Now here he was inside the shop looking at the fancy dress costumes, the tricks, the toys, the crackers, all in a delicious jumble – an Aladdin's cave of fun.

His torch light picked out the different colours like a kaleidoscope. Bernie, the gang leader, had asked him to get tricks and jokes; things they could sell at school. It was after finding these and stuffing as many as he could inside his jumper that he saw the masks.

They cascaded down from the ceiling, dozens of them, attached to a green pegboard backing: bulbous red cheeks; deformed noses; blank eye sockets; chalk-white foreheads – each one different, yet similar in ugliness.

Tom decided to take one for Trick or Treat Night. His torch picked out one in the middle. It was bigger than the rest. It had ginger-red hair on the top, a huge green forehead, deep-set eye sockets, puffed-out, blotchy cheeks, and a long curled-up nose. But, worst of all, was its grin – fat purple lips stretching in a twisted grimace. Stubs of rotting teeth hung from its upper lip. Tufts of the same ginger hair sprouted from its chin which stuck out like a Mr Punch.

Tom was fascinated with the mask. His heart slowed. He let his torch play on it. He did not hear the others outside urging him to hurry. He put out a finger and touched its nose.

SCREECH!

A long, green tongue shot out of the grimacing mouth and touched his own nose. It was like one of those things you find in crackers and blow at a friend's ear. There for a moment it stuck like a limpet. From the mouth came a sweet, sooty smell. Tom cried out and flailed his arms to detach the tentacle tongue. As he did so masks tumbled from the stand and bounced round his feet like rubber balls.

He had a momentary glimpse of an eye in the left socket. Crying out he rushed for the lavatory window still flailing his arms as he could feel something sucking on his nose. He went through the window and fell headlong into a pile of cardboard boxes. Jokes and tricks fell out of his jumper and littered the yard. His mates, hearing his cries inside, had fled.

He scrambled over the yard wall and ran into the street still flailing his arms. As he turned into it he glanced back. There was the mask, floating above the yard wall in the orange light of a sodium lamp. He put his head down and ran.

Now he was in the High Street. Thank goodness there were people there, walking home, lit by shop windows. He ran the full length of the street dodging them. At the end he glanced behind him. There was the mask, lit by a shop window, on top of a pillar-box.

Rain began to fall. Tom darted round the corner. His flat was 2 miles away. He ran across the Green. Branches arched over him like black cobwebs. And there, as the moon came from behind a rain cloud, was the mask leering down at him. He tore across the grass and into the High Street again. Thankfully a bus drew up. He leapt on.

'Trying to break a record,' said the driver as Tom's chest billowed up and down.

He raced up the stairs to a back seat, hardly daring to turn his head. But when he did so there was the mask, over the traffic lights, its face changing colour with them; its glow reflected in the wet tarmac. He half cried out. A couple sitting up ahead of him turned round. He jumped downstairs. The driver eyed him suspiciously. Each time the bus stopped and the door hissed open he felt vulnerable.

When the bus finally stopped at his stop he leapt off and, head down, ran for his flat. But his legs felt weak and he stumbled over the uneven paving.

He rushed up the stairs to his flat, too afraid to wait for the lift. He had to will his legs to work.

The flat was in darkness. His mother and father were out at the club. He made sure the door was locked and took a hurried drink of Coca Cola. Then he went to the window and slowly opened a chink in the curtains. There was the mask, hovering over the garages like a clown dancing on the roofs.

He rushed into his bedroom and hid under the blankets. His heart hammered away. His parents could be an hour yet. He shook violently. He could not look out of the window again. He could not leave his bed.

To his relief his parents came in within ten minutes. He did not get up. He could not tell them of his fear. Opening his eyes he could see the shape of the mask in the pattern of the curtains as they moved in the wind. Then he drifted off into a fitful sleep in which the mask came and went, drifting as a bird in a thermal current.

At one moment the mask was far away, then it was close to him. Now it was swooping down like a giant eagle and the green tongue shot out! He awoke with a cry. It was not the tongue on his cheek but his mother's hand.

'You've got a temperature, love. I've been up to you three times in the night. Crying out you were. It's the doctor for you.'

Tom twisted and turned. Would the doctor say he was mad? He sobbed into the pillow. His mother brought him in a drink. 'Come on, open your eyes,' she said. What would he see when he opened them? Would the mask be there in the room? He dragged them open. His mother had drawn the curtains. He could see no mask, but it was still strong in his mind's eye.

The doctor came. He was a young locum. 'It's a virus, I should think,' he said. He did not sound too sure.

'What is that rash on his nose?' asked his mother.

To the doctor it looked like a snake bite but he said. 'I should think he has scratched himself in his sleep. You said he was very restless in the night. You haven't been with any pets or animals?' he asked.

'No,' mumbled Tom.

'He must stay in bed. Probably for a week. I'll look in tomorrow,' he said. 'This prescription will bring his temperature down.' He left resolving to look in his medical books when he got home.

In the shop yard an old man surveyed the jokes and tricks among the cardboard boxes. Then he looked up at the smashed window. He let himself in.

Inside he looked around. A smile came on his face as he looked at the masks. He patted the big ginger-haired one in the middle. His mail was on the coconut mat. He picked up a buff envelope. Just a circular for burglar alarms. He tore it up. Then he took down a black book from the shelf above his desk chuckling as he did so.

Think It Over

1 Why was Tom in the shop?
2 How were the masks displayed?
3 What was ugly about the mask?
4 How did Tom leave the shop?
5 When did he first see the mask following him?

6 Where was the mask in the High Street?
7 Why did Tom leap on the bus?
8 Why did he not feel safe even on the bus?
9 What did he do when he arrived home?
10 Why did his mother get up in the night?
11 Why was the doctor uncertain about Tom's illness?

Think It Out

1 Why is the term 'Aladdin's cave' used?
2 What is devilish about the mask?
3 Why was he afraid even in a crowd?
4 When do you first know that he is ill?
5 Did the mask really follow him?
6 Why did the doctor ask about pets and why will he consult his medical books?
7 What is the significance of the 'black book'?

Using Words

1 Use these words in sentences of your own as they are normally used
cascaded; billowed.
2 What different meanings have these words:
watch; sprout; crackers; buff.
3 What 'colour' words are important to the story? How do they help its atmosphere?

Discuss Now

How far should shopkeepers go to discourage thieves?
What makes this a frightening story?

Write Now

1 What words would you use to describe the atmosphere in these shops: a pharmacist's; a greengrocer's; a butcher's?
2 When he is delirious Tom has another dream. Describe it.
3 Write, as a play, what Tom tells Bernie when he recovers.

Mrs Speckley

Funnily enough, the moment I saw old Mrs Speckley, I thought of ferrets. She has very short hair, greyish brown, growing on her flat skull, and tiny, brilliant eyes which dart this way and that. Her skinny body in that long sand-coloured overcoat of hers, also, for me, had some of a ferret's snaky slinkiness. Rex is much the same.

I did mention it to Bert Thomson and one or two others in the pub which might not have been wise. It's not a good thing in Durklington to be too free in comment about its people. Everybody there is someone else's relation. One big family, so to speak, except for us 'settlers'.

That's because there's only one way out of the village. It's been left to itself for years – centuries even – until recently when we settlers started to arrive. That's what they call people like me who come from outside to live.

I saw it first in summer with its small, crooked houses clustering together like old women whispering secrets and the dark trees round the graveyard reaching out fingers of shadow in the bright sun towards the church. It was then I fell under its spell and bought a cottage.

In winter I saw it differently.

It was an autumn day when I met Mrs Speckley. I hadn't been living in the village very long and I was going to take a stroll through the woods of Skelling Copse. There's a stile that takes you in there from the road. Mrs Speckley and Rex were just coming out of the wood. I stood aside politely from the stile to let them pass and said, 'Good afternoon.' They didn't answer but only shot me keen glances from their bright little eyes. Rex showed his teeth.

I don't know why I mentioned it in the pub that night. I wasn't trying to stir up trouble for anyone. I just wanted to enquire.

'I thought it was against the law to catch pheasants,' I said.

'It is,' Bert Thomson told me. He was one of the villagers willing to talk to a settler like me. 'Why ask?' he added.

'I went for a walk in Skelling Copse today,' I explained, 'and met Mrs Speckley. She was carrying a pheasant and two rabbits. Rex, her son, had a ferret in its cage.'

'Her son?' said 'Taddy' Willows, another villager, standing next to us at the bar. He'd never spoken to me before.

'He's not her son,' said Bert Thomson gruffly.

'No,' Taddy agreed. 'He came here as a visitor like you.'

'Been here a fair while now,' said another man, a stranger to me.

'Got sort of bitten by the place,' another added. The three exchanged looks. Their faces were blank. I couldn't tell what they were thinking. It made me uneasy. That made me talkative.

'The gamekeeper lets her take a pheasant now and again, eh?' I asked.

'He'd better,' Taddy told me and the three men smiled without humour.

'Doesn't do to talk too much about it,' Bert Thomson muttered warningly and I changed the subject.

A few days later I saw Mrs Speckley again making for Skelling Copse. Rex wasn't with her. In the cage she carried were two ferrets.

79

I'm not the only 'settler' in Durklington. There's old Mr Tennant and an elderly married couple whose name I don't know. They keep themselves to themselves. Then there's Mrs Flaxton, a widow in her late fifties, who lives alone. She used to make her presence felt in the village but she's drawn in her horns recently. That began about the time she started the arguments with Mrs Speckley.

There's quite a bit of land which goes with Mrs Flaxton's bungalow. It's rough and part of it is a rabbit warren. I was passing there one day when I heard Mrs Flaxton shout, 'Hello! Hey! You there!'

I looked, wondering whether she was shouting at me. Then I saw Mrs Speckley and Rex coming down the field. Mrs Speckley was carrying two dead rabbits. Rex had the cage. It had one ferret in it.

'What do you think you're doing?' Mrs Flaxton called in her commanding, well-educated voice. They came tripping stealthily down the field and stopped, looking at her. The ferret circled its cage, moving and nodding its head from side to side.

'Rabbiting, dearie,' said Mrs Speckley. She writhed her neck a bit as she spoke.

'Not on my land, you're not,' boomed Mrs Flaxton. 'You're trespassing and poaching. Get off my field or you'll find yourselves in trouble with the law.'

'Not too much of that round here, dearie,' Mrs Speckley told her in her thin, squeaky voice. Rex had opened the field gate and the two went off, quite unconcerned.

'What a dreadful woman!' Mrs Flaxton exclaimed, zipping up her smart, dark-yellow anorak which she had evidently pulled on as she rushed out of the bungalow. She had always been a bit distant towards me. Now she was obviously glad to have someone to talk to. I made an encouraging noise, I really did feel quite sympathetic. There was a swaggering air of triumph about Mrs

Speckley that I didn't like at all.

'And, do you know, that – that fellow with her used to be a school teacher,' Mrs Flaxton went on. 'Mr Thomson told me about him.'

I knew Bert Thomson did gardening for her.

'They used to be at daggers drawn at one time, Mr Thomson said,' she continued.

'A school teacher?' I interrupted, surprised.

'He rented a cottage. Stayed here at weekends and during school holidays. He had a cat he brought with him until that villainous ferret of Mrs Speckley's killed it. Then they had a stand up row round at her place. He got hold of the ferret in a rage and it bit him. It was all over the village at the time, Mr Thomson said. Then the fellow changed.'

'How?' I asked.

'Well, you can see for yourself,' she snorted. 'It didn't just blow over. He did more than cave in. Fell completely under her power. He's moved in with her to live. They're as thick as thieves.'

She had a lot more to say but it's that bit of conversation that sticks in my mind.

The quarrel didn't stop there. Mrs Speckley went on putting ferrets down the warren in Mrs Flaxton's field and netting rabbits until Mrs Flaxton really lost her temper. By all accounts, she grabbed the cage one day and tried to choke the ferret that was in it. She simply got bitten. She had to go into Norford, the nearest town, to see a doctor who gave her an injection. But she didn't take legal action and though Rex and Mrs Speckley didn't stop trespassing and trapping in her field, Mrs Flaxton seemed to have lost heart.

It never occurred to me that there might be something very strange going on even when I saw the ferret run into Mrs Flaxton's bungalow.

I often went past there. It was my favourite walk. It was quite a big animal, larger than the two I had seen in Mrs Speckley's cage. It had a different-coloured coat, too, a dirty yellow. It was a warm day; Mrs Flaxton's door was wide open. The ferret glided in there.

I stopped, expecting to hear a scream or something but Mrs Flaxton came out almost immediately.

'Did you see the ferret?' I called and went up the garden path to her.

'I must have been asleep for hours,' she said crossly, looking a bit dazed. She hadn't heard my question. She muttered on about some dream she'd had. I could hardly hear that. Was it really about her threading her way through tunnels, chasing something and raw meat? She seemed only half aware that I was there but when I asked her if she was all right she pulled herself together.

'Perfectly all right, thank you,' she said sharply and went in, closing the door behind her with a snap.

Last week it all came together to make a pattern in my mind. I've had six bantam hens in a little pen at the back of my cottage for about two months. That Friday I came out to see the ferret at them. It fled when it saw me, through the hedge, and disappeared up the road. It left two bantams dead.

I didn't think, I was in such a rage. The bantams never had laid well but I was very fond of them. I picked up one of the bodies. I don't even remember stamping down that back lane to Mrs Speckley's place. I went in. She was there alone. The room was tidy in the way that an animal's lair is tidy but there was a pungent, acrid smell in the air. There was no sign of any ferret. I shook the dead bantam in her face. I can't remember what I said.

I do remember the way she poked her head viciously forward. Her eyes glittered, her sharp nose and small mouth seemed to draw together in a point.

'You'll be sorry about this,' she spat. 'Calling names! Been talking bad about me, too, up and down, ain't you? Think you're safe with Rex and the ferret away. But I could fix you myself. Here. Right now.'

Her head darted again at me and she showed her teeth. I drew back. It was almost as if she were about to bite me. Then I noticed something. She had whiskers on her chin and around her lips.

It could have floated there off the bantam I had brandished. On the other hand, it could have been picked up off one of the squawking bantams in my back yard. I did certainly see a tiny white feather fluttering on her hairy upper lip. The sight filled me with a sudden dreadful thought. I blundered straight out of her house.

This is the eighth day I've been in this guest house in Bristol. I only stopped in Durklington long enough to ask Bert Thomson to feed my remaining bantams while I was away.

Half my mind tells me I'm being ridiculous. It's incredible to think that Mrs Spreckley could change a school teacher – or anyone – into an animal which is human part of the time. It's unbelievable that Mrs Flaxton had become a ferret-lady.

And yet – why can't I rid myself of this feeling that something quite terrible might happen to me, if I go back to Durklington?

Think It Over

1 When the storyteller saw Mrs Speckley for the first time what did she remind him of?
2 To whom did he talk about that?
3 What had first attracted him to come and live in the village?
4 Which woman in the village had an argument with Mrs Speckley?
5 What was the argument about?

83

6 What colour was Mrs Flaxton's anorak?
7 What job had Rex done before he came to the village?
8 What had happened to him after he had had an argument with Mrs Speckley?
9 What colour was the ferret that ran into Mrs Flaxton's house?
10 What had Mrs Flaxton been dreaming about?
11 Why did the storyteller quarrel with Mrs Speckley?
12 What odd thing did he see among the hairs on Mrs Speckley's lip?
13 Where did he go almost immediately after quarrelling with her?
14 What does he think might happen to him if he goes back to Durklington?

Think It Out

1 Why might it not be wise to criticise one person to another in Durklington?
2 When the storyteller and Rex met for the first time, Rex 'showed his teeth'. Was he smiling or not? Say why you think so.
3 Why do you think the gamekeeper allowed Mrs Speckley to poach pheasants?
4 Name three things about Mrs Speckley that are ferret like.
5 What do you think Mrs Speckley did to make Rex fall 'completely under her power'?
6 What seems to have happened to Mrs Flaxton after her last quarrel with Mrs Speckley?
7 Why might the storyteller have seen no ferret in Mrs Speckley's house, when he went to complain about the killing of his bantam hen?

Using Words

1 Punctuate as speech:
he's not her son said Bert Thomson gruffly no Taddy agreed he come here as a visitor like you been here a fair while now said another man a stranger to me got sort of bitten by the place another added.
2 'She used to make her presence felt in the village but she's

drawn in her horns recently.'
Explain in your own words the meaning of 'She used to make her presence felt' and 'she's drawn in her horns'.
3 Rabbits live in a warren. Match up the following animals with the places where they live:
squirrel; eagle; badger; hare; fox; earth; lair; drey; nest; form
4 What law are you breaking if you are trespassing? What are you doing if you are poaching?
5 'She had always been a bit distant towards me.' How had she behaved?
6 What kind of smell is 'acrid'?

Discuss Now

Should game birds, like pheasants and grouse, be kept so that people who can pay for it are allowed to shoot them? Or should anyone who wishes to be allowed to shoot such birds? Is the hunting of foxes or deer or otters necessary for their preservation? Or are the rearing and shooting of game birds and hunting generally out of place in a modern society? To make a sinister story, you need a sinister setting, sinister characters or both. But they must not be blatantly sinister, not too obvious. What is disturbing about the village in which the story is set? What is sinister about Mrs Speckley? What kinds of places would you choose for a sinister story?

Try making up a sinister story in groups of four. One person should then tell the story to the whole class.

Write Now

1 Write your own story about someone who can change or who is changed into an animal. It could be yourself. You could choose an animal you liked. It could be a comic or serious story.
2 'Tom Fell had been poaching pheasants again. This time, Jack Benson, the gamekeeper was determined to catch him.' Did he succeed or was Tom Fell too smart for him? Finish the story.
3 In play form write the scene where Rex complains to Mrs Speckley about the killing of his cat.

The Exterminator

The alien space ship orbited Earth several times, scanning the planet, before it landed. In that dim and distant past, there were few man-like animals. The beings in the ship saw none.

They landed in the Arctic. One of them drilled a deep round hole in the ice. When it was finished, two others carried something out of the ship. To Earth eyes, it would have looked like a globe of whirling blackness. They lowered it carefully into the hole and packed the ice thickly on top of it again.

'Finished,' said one.

'Not before time,' agreed another. 'It nearly wiped out our race.'

'And our planet,' said the third. 'Even here it will not die.'

'The forcefield will keep it safe,' said the first, 'and the ice will hold it fast.'

The space ship blazed like a fading star in the sky as it disappeared. Only the animals that lived in the ages before man, were there to see it go.

There were five people on the sailing boat. Richard Green was there because he was a fully experienced sailor. Alan Todd had invited him along to keep them all out of trouble. Rose Todd had been doubtful, but not because she thought Green didn't know his job. She just thought he was not an easy man to get along with. She kept her opinions to herself, however. Mary Weston, her friend, and Don Weston, Mary's husband, were the least experienced of the crew. They were glad of the chance Alan had given them of a long, pleasant ocean voyage and they were anxious to please.

They had picked the boat up in Lisbon and were making for the Azores. Alan had chartered it and paid most of the cost. Don had made his smaller contribution. Richard had only paid for his share of the food. Alan had maintained that Richard's skill in piloting the boat was worth a lot.

It was a comfortable boat. They were a good way out from Lisbon. The weather had been kind to them. All of them were enjoying the voyage.

After breakfast that morning, Alan was struck with a sudden idea. They were under sail and making good speed. The sky was almost cloudless and the breeze made the warmth of the sun pleasant. Richard Green was at the helm.

'Fishing?' he objected. 'You want to leave to do some fishing?'

'Why not?' said Alan. 'There's no sign of any bad weather. We can spare the time.'

Richard argued that they should take advantage of conditions and sail on to make a lot of distance that day. Alan, though, was set on fishing and he was the boss.

A huge earth tremor that year had cracked ice in the Arctic that had not moved for thousands of years. Blocks broke off and moved out into the summer sea. Two or three bergs began to move south, melting. The thing inside one of them floated free; warmer waters carried it further south, stirring it into dull life.

On the boat, they took in sail, put out a sea anchor and Don and Alan fished while Rose and Mary chatted and Richard either sat about in moody silence or occupied himself with small jobs in the cabin.

It took about 2 hours for Alan and Don to have enough

of the sport. They hadn't caught many fish but they had enough to make a meal for them all in the evening.

They never ate it. Late that afternoon, Richard Green went mad.

It began quietly enough. Alan was steering. Rose, Mary and Don were sitting with him in the cockpit. Richard was down below. From time to time Mary could see him moving about in the cabin down there.

They all stopped talking when they heard the crash. The crunching, ripping sounds went on. Mary, who couldn't quite see what was happening, put her head down into the cabin doorway.

'Richard!' they heard her shout. 'What are you doing?' She turned back to them all, her face a mask of shock. 'He's smashing the radio!' she gasped.

'He's – what?' Don brushed her aside. Before he could go down the steps to the cabin, Richard came up them, snarling at him, carrying a knife. Don grappled with him but Richard tore himself free and stabbed him in the side. Don hung on bravely.

'Alan!' he choked and, as Alan went to help him, Mary screamed.

With no one at the helm, the wind took the boat and it rolled and rocked sickeningly before it came up into the wind. Rose did her best to control it but she had to protect herself against the struggling bodies that swayed and fought from side to side in the lurching cockpit.

Alan and Don got Richard under control at last and, with Mary's help, they tied up his arms and legs. Then they lashed him to one of the bunks in the cabin. They had shouted at him in the struggle, trying to bring him back to his senses. Richard had not said a word but growled like an animal. Now he lay silent in the bunk, staring up at them with bright, mad eyes.

Don suddenly sat back on the other bunk, groaning. He showed them his scarlet hands. The front of his shirt was red with blood.

'He got me twice,' he said in a surprised whisper. He would have collapsed head first forward if Mary and Alan had not caught him and laid him gently in the bunk.

They let the boat yaw and sway while they did what they could for him. They were interrupted by Richard who began to fight the ropes that held him, tugging at them with surprising strength and muttering gibberish. Alan gave him an injection from the medical supplies and knocked him out.

Don was not too uncomfortable by the time he was bandaged and had regained consciousness. His pain started about an hour after dark and he had to be given a painkilling shot, too.

Alan had already set the boat back on a course for Lisbon. The steering was taking up much of his attention. They were sailing into the wind which meant periodic changes of course. They did, in fact, have plenty of fuel but not enough to turn on the engine there and then and motor all the way back.

Mary, who had just checked on Don's condition, joined Alan and Rose in the cockpit. 'I hope he'll be all right.' Her voice trembled and cracked but she mastered it. 'Awful!' she said.

'Richard must have been a bit crazy all the time,' Rose decided. 'I never really trusted him.'

'Less crazy than most,' Alan objected. 'I've been sailing with him in all sorts of weathers. He's never shown a sign of anything like this before. I don't know what's got into him.'

'Nothing 'got into him,' ' Mary protested angrily. 'He's violent – dangerous. If anything happens to Don . . .'

She was wrong. Something had got into Richard.

Alone, it was neither living nor dead. It needed life to feed on. It could take living creatures and draw strength from them. It could take from them memory and intelligence and grow in knowledge. Still only half alive, it realised that Richard's body, as a prisoner, was of little use to it. So it moved on.

'What was that?' Rose stared into the dimness of the cabin.

'I didn't see anything.' Alan peered, too. They had left a low light down there.

'I could swear I saw something scuttle across the floor,' she said.

'Take the helm,' he told her. 'I'll have a look.'

She did so. She and Mary waited as Alan turned up the light in the cabin and inspected the place. He looked up at them at last from the doorway and shook his head.

'Nothing,' he said. 'Richard's still out cold. Don, too. He seems comfortable.' He frowned, biting his lip. Then he shook his head and stepped back. They could hear him move away to the forward cabin. A drawer opened and closed. He came back again, turning down the light, and climbed up into the cockpit. As he took the helm, Rose asked, 'What were you looking for?'

'Just checking,' he said. She wondered. He had taken something from the drawer. She could see the slight bulge of it, hidden in the front of his shirt.

Mary shivered suddenly, though the night was warm.

'I've got the weirdest feeling,' she said.

'So have I,' Rose murmured. 'It's just as if there's someone else extra on the boat.'

'Now, don't start imagining things,' Alan warned crisply. Rose, however, noticed that from time to time he would take his eyes from the compass or the sails to take a hard look down into the semi-darkness of the cabin.

They decided that Mary would take the first watch on deck, steering the ship. Rose would take the second. Alan, too, would stay on deck, getting what rest he could her way to look at the two men in the bunks. From the cockpit they heard her cry out in surprise. Then she came quickly back up the steps.

'Richard,' she said.

'Giving trouble?' asked Alan.

'He's dead,' she whispered.

'Take the helm,' he ordered and went below. She was right. There was no pulse in Richard's neck. In the light of Alan's torch, the dead face was waxy, pale as chalk. It was much thinner than Alan remembered it, almost skull-like, with closed eyes sunk deep in their sockets and the cheeks fallen in. He stared at it for a long minute. Then he turned to Don, was reassured by his quiet breathing, and went back up on deck.

'I don't know how it could have happened,' he said slowly.

'And Don?' asked Mary anxiously.

'He's sleeping easily,' he told her.

'What are we going to do about it?' asked Rose. They discussed it in low, worried voices. If possible, they ought to take Richard back for medical examination. The weather, though, was hot. They had no way of preserving the body. They might have to bury it at sea.

'We shall have to leave it till morning,' Alan decided at last. 'You'd better get what sleep you can, Rose.'

Rose, reluctantly, went down again. Alan curled up on a seat in the cockpit. Both of them felt too nervous and wide awake to rest. The day's events had taken it out of them, though. After 20 minutes, they were both fast asleep.

It lay on the bunk, using its new-found ability to think. It had drawn strength and knowledge from its first host body. It had realised it could be greater than a sir. of these creatures. They were individually weak. body it was now in was both weak and injured. But i. too weak to be useless. It could move.

The mind behind Don's closed eyes was still not fully alive. Now, though, it could use human speech and human skills. It knew what it was and what it could do. It could grow and spread to include numberless human beings in its web. And, with every mind it reached out for and possessed, it would grow in power.

Mary, drowsily steering, realised she must have been half-dozing. She had not heard him come up the steps.

'Don?' she hesitated, not sure whether his appearance in the dark cockpit meant that he had recovered or not. Then she flinched in sudden disgust. 'Aagh!' For an instant she thought that the clot of blacker shadow falling from his mouth was blood until it flashed towards her. It struck her face, momentarily agonising as it penetrated like needles. Then there was nothing.

Alan, coming muzzily out of nightmare, had hardly time to set his feet on the deck. He was reaching for the gun he had put in the front of his shirt when white fire invaded his brain, destroying him. Rose, asleep below, did not even have time to know what had happened to her.

Alan was steering. Rose and Mary sat with him in the cockpit. Don's dead body and Richard's lay on the bunks down in the cabin. The mind that had been a prisoner in the ice looked out of three pairs of human eyes. It knew nearly everything now. Shortly it would turn on the engine. They would make better speed back to land. That was necessary. These bodies would not endure for long. Their strength did not last. Feeding the thing's power, they were soon drained. But it was not anxious. In two or three days it would reach land. Then there would be a continent of people to serve its needs.

Think It Over

1. What did the thing carried out of the aliens' spaceship look like?
2. What had it done on the alien planet?
3. From which port had the party on the boat set out?
4. Why did Alan want to stop the boat?
5. How had the thing imprisoned in the Arctic ice freed itself?
6. What was the first sign of Richard Green's 'madness'?
7. How did Don get hurt?
8. What did they do to Richard when he struggled against the ropes?
9. What did Rose think she saw in the dark of the cabin?
10. What sudden feeling about the boat did Mary and Rose have?
11. Who discovered Richard's death?
12. Which body did the alien creature first use when it left Richard?
13. Where did it move to after that?
14. Where was it at the end of the story?

Think It Out

1. What, apart from the ice, held the alien thing prisoner?
2. When did the creature come on to the boat?
3. Why might it, through Richard Green, have smashed the radio?
4. Why might it have been wild and savage at first and calmer later?
5. How do you know that Alan, too, fears that there is something on the boat with them?
6. What suggests that the alien has in some way 'fed' on Richard?
7. What, at the end of the story, suggests that people in Europe are in danger?

Using Words

1. What do you understand by 'a force field'?

93

2. In what country is Lisbon and where are the Azores?
3. '... he was not an easy man to get along with.' What does that suggest about the way he usually behaved towards other people?
4. What does a ship do if it 'heaves to'?
5. What is the helm on a boat used for?
6. What are 'periodic changes'?
7. 'Alan!' he choked.
   Find four other words, apart from 'said', which show how one of the characters spoke.

Discuss Now

In films and stories there are beings from other worlds. Some people do, in fact, believe that there are such things as UFOs. Is there any real scientific evidence for such things? Has anyone in the discussion any evidence to offer? Or is there scientific evidence that such things cannot possibly exist?

Write Now

1. Write your own story about finding an object or meeting a being from another planet.
2. If you had all the money you needed, where would you go on holiday? Describe what you expect the place to be like and say what you would do there. Or write about the worst holiday you ever had. It could be a real or imaginary experience.
3. You are on an expedition into wild mountain country or into the jungle. Your guide seems very surly and unfriendly at first. Have you misjudged him? Does he turn out to be good when you run into danger? Or does he lead you into danger? Why is he surly? Write the story.
4. Continue the story of 'The Exterminator'. What happens when they get back to Lisbon. Are people suspicious of them because of the way they behave. Or does the alien creature take over more victims? If it is defeated in the end, how does this happen?

Thank You, Halley's Comet

You were disappointed by the appearance of Halley's Comet in 1986. In fact, I bet you didn't see it at all. I didn't. But I am glad it was there. Am I just.

I live in the small Somerset village of Newton Cherrill. More people have heard of that comet way out in space than our village here in England. It's a sleepy place. But in that year it became a more sleepy place, if you see what I mean. Well, you will in a minute.

I first met Mr Smith down Rudyard's Lane next to the common. I had a bit of a shock when this big bloke tapped me on the shoulder. One minute I was there, alone, in the lane, and the next minute there was this guy towering over me. Six foot six he was at least. He came out of the blue, as it were. He was carrying a blue metallic case. He looked very brown, just as if he were back from the Costa Brava.

'Can you direct me to some lodgings?' he said. He had a funny way of speaking, as though his voice came through a telephone.

Now it happened that Auntie Bet who I lived with did bed and breakfast. She was always keen on making an extra quid or two so I took him along. And I soon got to know him.

The funny voice was the result of a car accident, he said. He had come down from London to set up a little solar-heating factory. His firm wanted to try it out in a quiet way to keep their method secret and out of the eyes of their competitors.

Within a fortnight he had arranged to take over the old railway station as a workshop and he had persuaded me to go in with him. I worked at the local blacksmith's and he said he could use my skills. I could not see much future at the smithy though there was plenty of work with the horses. But I wanted to make my way in the world and see a bit of it that wasn't Newton Cherrill.

This bloke worked hard; in fact he never seemed to sleep. I could hear him pacing about his room at Aunt Bet's even after a twelve-hour day.

We had soon made ten of these units. They were about a metre square and made of copper. He coated them with a liquid he had in tins in his metal case. They were only little tins but this coating just spread and spread like old ink on a blotter. He would never tell me what it was. 'Industrial secret,' he would say, tapping his smooth chin.

He paid me well though, always in new notes. So I didn't bother over much. In the afternoons I had to go out and persuade people to let us fit them to their roofs. The first ten were free. But I had a bit of a job with the conservative villagers. Well, not many of them even had double-glazing.

But in the end, after me buying some of them a few pints at the pub, we got ten up. I plumbed them into the hot-water systems.

Good reports soon came in: lashings of hot water, all free, even on a dull day. They were all fitted facing south. Mr Smith did the fitting. He had a small machine like a compass to calculate the way they were facing. He said this was critical.

Orders from the rest of the village came tumbling in just by word of mouth. I expected him to take on more staff, but he didn't. He said he could trust me with the secrets. Not that he had told me any.

Within six months we had the whole village fitted up, except a few old dears who didn't seem to need hot water. Mr Smith got very excited. His skin sort of glowed purplish as if he needed a shave. I could see a big future in his firm for me, not that I had met anyone else in it.

Then came that day. I had had a few the night before. I was celebrating the installation of the hundredth unit. Mr Smith didn't drink: he said it upset his stomach. But he gave me a tenner to have a drink with the lads.

When I woke up next morning my head throbbed and I felt in a daze. I thought the lads had slipped a whisky or two into my beer and I was cursing them. It's hard to describe: it was as though I was seeing things through a lens of a slow motion camera. I went downstairs, carefully picking my way down as though I was climbing down a mountain. Aunt Bet was in the kitchen. She said nothing to me but was having difficulty breaking the eggs into the frying pan. Mr Smith was down but he was moving about at a normal rate. He had earphonelike things on his head and a kind of aerial sticking up from a helmet. He kept smiling at us and patting us as though we were pets. I tried to talk to him but my tongue couldn't get round the words.

We ate our breakfast as best we could. I had trouble finding my mouth to put the food in. There was more on the tablecloth and on the floor than in my stomach.

Afterwards Mr Smith led us out onto the village square. He went in all the houses and got people out. We looked at each other but could not speak. He lined us up and made us do things like pick up stones and sweep the road. We were like a slow-moving chain gang.

Gradually we got better at doing things. We had learnt to adjust to the slower rate, though the old ones fell over a lot. I looked up at the roofs. The units we had fitted were crackling and sending out a bluey glow. Then Mr

97

Smith led us all home.

The next thing I remember was that I was on my way to work. Aunt Bet was giving me my packed lunch and we were talking as normal. I passed villagers as I biked to the factory but no-one said anything about the strange happening. It was as if it had been a dream. The time was ten to eight. It must have been a nightmare. I put it down to the booze.

At the factory Mr Smith was rushing about excitedly. He said the time had now come for the expansion. He had got his orders from Head Office.

I did not see him for the rest of the morning. I worked away on the copper plates. At lunch-time I knocked on his office door. I thought he might break his rules and have one at the local. There was no answer so I went in. There he was slumped over his desk. He was wearing the earphones and aerial thing I had seen in the 'dream'. He was running with sweat.

I got him home in Fred Arnold's taxi. And there in Aunt Bet's bedroom he gasped out this story to me. It went like this:

'I come from Franos in another galaxy – we have observed Planet Earth – we set up a space station in high orbit around it – from there we can send the emma rays to the receiving panels – the solar panels – and we can control the people – then we can take over – our base was to have been Cherrill Newton common – there we could land the space ships – none of your weapons could hurt us – the emma rays would protect – we could form a bridgehead for taking over the planet – but Halley's Comet – it was in the same orbit – it hit us this morning – I am no longer receiving the immunity ray – I will die of your flu – I will die in one minute . . .'

He groaned. Then he went cold and rigid. He was dead.

They did an autopsy on him. I had to go to a Whitehall office in London. It was way underground. I had to tell them about Mr Smith. They told me to say nothing to anybody or else I might disappear one night.

The papers said nothing except that shortly after Mr Smith's death there was a big meeting at the United Nations of all the world's top leaders. They said it was about peace.

The local paper also said something about a burnt patch on the common and some queer bits of metal but they reckoned it was a meteorite or ball lightning.

Anyway I've written the story down. I'm putting it in a metal box of mine – the one Mr Smith left. Someone will look in it after my death. That is, if I live my time out – or any of us lives our time out in life as we know it. You see, I keep looking up into the sky and wondering about Franos.

Think It Over

1. Where does the story take place?
2. What was odd about the meeting of the narrator and Mr Smith?
3. What did Mr Smith want?
4. How did Mr Smith explain the funny voice?
5. What did he plan to do at Newton Cherrill?
6. Where did they set up the factory?
7. What was odd about the content of the tins?
8. Why were there so many orders in the village?
9. How did the narrator feel when he woke up after the night in the pub?
10. Who else was affected?
11. What were the units doing?
12. What caused Franos's plan to go wrong?
13. Why did Mr Smith die?

Think It Out

1. What do we learn about the narrator?
2. Why might the visitor be called Mr Smith?
3. What possible evidence is there before his revelation, that Mr Smith comes from another planet?
4. Why was this particular village picked?
5. What might the small machine like a compass be?
6. What might be affecting the villagers?
7. Why would there be a meeting of the United Nations?
8. What effect could this have on future world relations?

Using Words

1. When do people use these words: *lodgings; digs; accommodation; board*?
2. Write the plurals of these words: *roof; hoof; loaf.*
3. Write these out as words: *100th; 50th; 20th; 40th.*
4. Use *slip* in three different ways in sentences of your own.

Discuss Now

Was the narrator a fool not to suspect something?
Is there any evidence of life on other planets?
Do you agree that there is much less interest in Space Travel than there was? Can you suggest reasons why this might be so?
The cost of Space exploration is enormous. Do you think the money could be better spent? On what?

Write Now

1. You are on Newton Cherrill common. You see Mr Smith arrive in a small spaceship. Describe your experience.
2. You then go to the local police station with this news and are regarded as an idiot. Write, as a play, your interview with a police sergeant.
3. The 'solar' panels must be removed from the houses, although they work perfectly well. Draft a letter from the Government that is sent to each householder. What reasons could be given without telling the truth.